Land Reform in Brazil: The Management of Social Change

Marta Cehelsky

Routledge
Taylor & Francis Group
LONDON AND NEW YORK

First published 1979 by Westview Press

Published 2018 by Routledge
52 Vanderbilt Avenue, New York, NY 10017
2 Park Square, Milton Park, Abingdon, Oxon OX14 4RN

Routledge is an imprint of the Taylor & Francis Group, an informa business

Library of Congress Catalog Card Number: 79-3974
ISBN: 0-89158-075-1

ISBN 13: 978-0-367-02066-8 (hbk)
ISBN 13: 978-0-367-17053-0 (pbk)

To Michael R. and Irene Cehelsky

Land Reform in Brazil

Westview Replica Editions

This book is a Westview Replica Edition. The concept of Replica Editions is a response to the crisis in academic and informational publishing. Library budgets for books have been severely curtailed; economic pressures on the university presses and the few private publishing companies primarily interested in scholarly manuscripts have severely limited the capacity of the industry to properly serve the academic and research communities. Many manuscripts dealing with important subjects, often representing the highest level of scholarship, are today not economically viable publishing projects. Or, if they are accepted for publication, they are often subject to lead times ranging from one to three years. Scholars are understandably frustrated when they realize that their first-class research cannot be published within a reasonable time frame, if at all.

Westview Replica Editions are our practical solution to the problem. The concept is simple. We accept a manuscript in camera-ready form and move it immediately into the production process. The responsibility for textual and copy editing lies with the author or sponsoring organization. If necessary we will advise the author on proper preparation of footnotes and bibliography. We prefer that the manuscript be typed according to our specifications, though it may be acceptable as typed for a dissertation or prepared in some other clearly organized and readable way. The end result is a book produced by lithography and bound in hard covers. Initial edition sizes range from 400 to 600 copies, and a number of recent Replicas are already in second printings. We include among Westview Replica Editions only works of outstanding scholarly quality or of great informational value, and we will continue to exercise our usual editorial standards and quality control.

Land Reform in Brazil: The Management of Social Change

Marta Cehelsky

Land reform stands as one of the most explosive issues in modern Brazil. Having contributed to the downfall of João Goulart's populist democracy and to the establishment of an authoritarian regime, it became, ironically, an early major policy objective of the new military government.

This volume documents the disintegration of Brazilian democracy and identifies the major reasons for its instability and its tendency to revert to authoritarian rule. Dr. Cehelsky explores the significance and treatment of land reform under democratic and authoritarian rule and assesses the overall impact of a measure originally intended to produce social reform. Viewed analytically, the management of the land reform issue in Brazil attests to the resilience of the traditional elites and their power to determine substantially the nature and rate of accommodation of social and economic change.

Marta Cehelsky is a policy analyst at NASA. She has taught political science at Brooklyn College and the University of Houston and has served as advisor to the commissioner of the U.S. Immigration and Naturalization Service.

Contents

Tables and Figures xi

Preface xiii

1 INTRODUCTION 1

Modernizing Authoritarianism 4

2 LAND, TRADITION, AND THE SOCIO-POLITICAL ORDER 15

Agrarian Society and Bureaucratic Patrimonial State 18

Rural Mobilization and Land Reform 33

3 PRESIDENTIAL POLITICS AND LAND REFORM 67

Agrarian Proposals 68

João Goulart and Land Reform 76

Castelo Branco and Land Reform 99

4 THE CONGRESSIONAL DEBATE: LEGISLATIVE POLITICS AND THE POLICY PROCESS 119

Political Parties and Interest Representation 122

Legislating Land Reform: João Goulart 130

5 POLITICAL BEHAVIOR AND THE LAND REFORM DEBATE 165

Regional and Economic Influences on Legislative Behavior 166

Political Party Affiliation and Attitudes Toward Land Reform 175

6 THE POLICY PROCESS AND CONSERVATIVE MODERNIZATION 197
Strategy and Style in Policy Making 198
The Land Statute of 1964 205
Agrarian Policy, 1965-1975 212
The Management of Change in Brazil 225

Appendix: Note on Sources 233
Glossary of Brazilian Terms and Acronyms 237
Bibliography 239
Index 253

Tables and Figures

Table

2-1 Relative Number and Area of Farm Units by Size of Group in CIDA Study Countries 38

2-2 Rural Occupational Structure, 1965 45

2-3 Membership, Brazilian Rural Confederation 50

3-1 Major Agrarian Legislation, 1960-1970 70

4-1 Brazilian Political Parties, 1945-1964 123

4-2 Distribution of Congressional Seats by Party, 1954-1960 126

5-1 States with High Levels of Participation in Agrarian Debate 172

5-2 Deputy Participation in Agrarian Reform Debate, by Party and by Year 178

5-3 Deputy Perception of Agrarian Problem, by Party 180

5-4 Relationship of Attitudes Toward an Agrarian Law and Attitudes Toward an Amendment: Distribution within Parties 182

5-5 Measure of Association between Attitudes on Need for Agrarian Reform and for Constitutional Amendment 183

5-6 Vote on the Constitutional Amendment 185

5-7 Willingness to Trust the Government with Agrarian Reform 187

5-8 Relationship of Attitude Toward President and Attitude Toward Amendment 188

5-9 Association Between Attitude Toward the Goulart-PTB Amendment, and Attitudes Toward Other Agrarian Bills 191

6-1 Structure of Authority Over Land Reform 219

Figure

5-1 Percentage of State Delegations Participating in Land Reform Debates 169

5-2 Regional Demographic Data and Deputy Participation in Chamber Debates 170

Preface

Throughout this book, Brazilian terms are frequently used in preference to imperfect English translations, or lengthy explanations. A glossary of such terms is provided for ready reference. Likewise, I adhere to the Brazilian custom of using first names or cognomen interchangeably with or in preference to family names. Thus, João Goulart is frequently referred to as Jango; Jânio Quadros as Jânio, etc. Also in keeping with common Brazilian usage, I refer to the overthrow of the Goulart administration in 1964 as the "revolution." This usage is a convenience and does not constitute a judgment of the true character of the event.

This book is a milestone in a Brazilian odyssey which began in senior year at Barnard College. Beginning with my senior thesis on the modern Brazilian presidency, observing and analyzing Brazilian politics -- its institutions, development, and leadership -- has been a source of constant fascination. Ronald Schnedier helped me take those first steps into the study of Brazil. For this and for his readiness over the years to share his extraordinary grasp and detailed knowledge of Brazilian politics and offer constant encouragement I owe him special gratitude.

In the course of preparing this book, I have benefitted from the help, advice, discussions, and critiques of many people. My largest debt is to the many Brazilians who have made it possible for me to study the politics of their country and share their insights. I promised confidentiality and anonymity to all individuals I interviewed, and therefore do not list them in the bibliography.

Sergio Bertoni, director of the cadastral department of the now defunct Brazilian Institute of Agrarian Reform, lent invaluable assistant in providing access to studies and documents prepared by his organization. José Felice, director of the *gaucho* branch of the Institute, did the same in Rio Grande do Sul. Amaro Cavalcanti and Ben Hur Raposo of the National Confederation of Agriculture provided documents and records on the activities of the CNA. Edgar Teixeira Leite, also an official of the CNA, generously opened up his personal library to me. General Golbery de Couto e Silva provided access to the archives of IPES, the Institute of Social Studies and Research. Manuel Diegues Júnior kindly helped with materials on rural problems in Brazil in the Centro Latino Americano de Pesquisas em Ciências Sociais.

Many of the sources I used for tracing the political debate on land reform are located in the Biblioteca Nacional, and in the library of the Fundação Getúlio Vargas. But special thanks for help in tracking down valuable sources and documents go to Roberto de Oliveria Campos, Paulo Assis Ribeiro, Raymundo Padilha, Assis Badra, João Cleofas, João Caruso, Thomas Pompeu Accioly Borges, and Aurélio Viana.

A grant from the Foreign Area Fellowship Program enabled me to research this project in Brazil. In the course of the research effort, I benefitted from discussions and helpful recommendations from Octavio Ianni, Gabriel Cohn, Juarez Rubens Brandão Lopez, Hélio Jaguaribe, Cândido Mendes de Almedia, Lauro Rangel, Philippe Schmitter, Kenneth Erickson, Anthony Leeds, Richard Graham, and Jonathan Dill. Alan Sager and Thomas Louis offered help on the processing of the debates in the Chamber of Deputies and Richard Moore helped with the coding.

Earlier drafts of this manuscript benefitted considerably from the thoughtful criticism of Dankwart Rustow, Douglas Chalmers, and Philip B. Taylor. To Doug Chalmers, and particularly to Dan Rustow, my intellectual debt extends well beyond the subject of this book.

Many have helped and contributed, often unknowingly, to this study, for which, of course, I bear final responsibility. No one, however, has borne the burden of it more or deserves more thanks than David T. Garza, my husband. He has been a fellow researcher, forum and critic for my ideas, and friend. Through many drafts he has provided unflagging moral support, the benefit of his insightful grasp of Brazilian politics and developmental problems, his keen editorial eye, and above all, his patience and sense of humor.

Finally, I thank Virginia Lyerly for her patience and dedication in the frequently trying task of putting this manuscript into its final typed form.

1. Introduction

This is a study of the struggle over land reform policy in Brazil during the 1960s. Its primary purpose is to provide insight into the workings of the Brazilian political system in general and the policy process in particular at a time when Brazil was undergoing a major crisis of regime. In this sense, this volume is not so much a study of agriculture and agrarian reform as it is a policy analysis in which land reform functions as an especially sensitive lens through which the workings of the political system can be examined. For this reason, matters such as rural social conditions and agricultural productivity are touched on only tangentially and for the limited purpose of providing a backdrop against which the agrarian struggle developed. Similarly, although the treatment of rural social structure and movements is more detailed, its primary purpose is to enhance our understanding of the impact of social actors on the policy process. Consequently, this is not primarily a study of peasant movements, or even, in any explicit sense, of rural development and politicization, although both have an important bearing on the issue. Discussion of the nature and significance of the Land Statute which was ultimately enacted by the military government in

1964, is undertaken more to assess its impact on the political system and on the distribution of power, rather than on rural development.

Still, the choice of agriculture as the focus of this study is not coincidental or casual, either from the perspective of the evolution of the Brazilian political order, or the crisis and upheaval of 1964 which terminated Brazilian democracy and replaced it with a military regime. Agriculture was the foundation of the Brazilian economy during colonial and early independence periods, and continues to be an important element of the economy, although the industrial sector has come to play an increasingly prominent role. Planter elites have occupied a central place in the traditional Brazilian political system, exercised considerable influence in that system, and contributed crucially to its stability, survival, and evolution. The modernizing transformation which began roughly in 1930 heralded Brazil's transition from an agrarian patrimonial political order to a modern authoritarian state. The revolution of 1964, in which the agrarian controversy played a prominent role, symbolized the initiation of the final phase of this transformation and centered on what Barrington Moore and others have indicated as the gravest of the modernizing hurdles -- that of incorporating the rural masses into the modern economy and political order.[1]

It is the specific intention of this study to place the examination of the land reform controversy in this broad political context and to offer some insight into the systemic importance of the issue. Although a central purpose of this volume is the reconstruction of the decision on land reform for the

1962-1970 period, the analysis is not restricted to the recreation of the major acts and scenarios of this agrarian policy drama, or to the recollection of memorable lines. Rather, the clarification of the policy mechanism, like a period piece, must be understood in relationship to the dynamics of the historical moment within which it is located and shaped. In addition to deriving its significance from this moment by throwing critical decisions and relationships into high relief, such analysis illuminates the context itself and lends it greater coherence. Also, since a policy decision contains not only the elements of a moral drama but also the possibilities of tragedy, its full appreciation is enhanced by discovering the historical roots of the event and its characters, and by locating the event itself within a meaningful developmental framework.

In relating the case study to historical roots, this volume attempts to provide some insight into the fundamental continuity of Brazil's political experience. To this end, the argument advanced in the succeeding pages goes beyond the observations of some recent writings which trace Brazil's current political institutions to Vargas' _Estado Nôvo_ some thirty years earlier.[2] While acknowledging the importance of the Vargas dictatorship for the development of political institutions, this study holds that there exists a far older traditional basis for the current institutional structure. Its specific characteristics were evident during the imperial period of early independence, and its origins rooted in the colonial era.[3] Despite the considerable impact of modernization, democratic ideologies, and political experimentation over time, Brazil has not yet undergone an experience basically transforming the traditional and authoritarian nature of its political order, or the primary institutional arrangements on which its has rested.

MODERNIZING AUTHORITARIANISM

This line of investigation is intended to shed additional light on a type of political system only recently singled out as worthy of independent study -- the authoritarian regime. In the 1960s, social scientific models of development, whether political or economic in emphasis, were predominently based on assumptions derived from the experiences of industrial, capitalist democracies. With these schemes, western scholars hoped to explain, and in some instances guide, the complex developmental processes of newly modernizing post-colonial nations. Totalitarian, or as I prefer to call them, collectivist state hegemonic regimes, the revolutionary progeny of developmental failures (it was assumed), were viewed as the major alternative to the western democratic tradition. With few exceptions, comparative developmental theorists paid relatively little attention to the distinct modernizing experience of older, traditional authoritarian systems. A strong assumption prevailed of their inherent instability and inability to manage and survive crises of economic and social change.

As these assumptions have failed to be borne out, scholars have begun to study more closely the persistent phenomenon of stable, authoritarian political orders.[4] Latin American nations and Spain and Portugal have become particularly important foci of interest for the study of authoritarian regimes and the process by which they undergo industrialization without sacrificing their traditional structures or institutions or succumbing to revolution.

Our theoretical understanding of these regimes, however, remains minimal. As Juan Linz has observed, we relegate them to a "residual" category.[5] The general recognition that conservative authoritarian regimes constitute a stable category apart from others has not automatically resulted in a definition of systemic traits shared by these nations. Furthermore, this lack of analytical clarity has occasioned some confusion as to which regimes fall into the residual category and how far. Linz, for example, suggests that Brazil, a major focal point for study of authoritarian politics, does not constitute an authoritarian regime, but an authoritarian "situation."[6] However, once one recognizes that a certain amount of political instability is characteristic of authoritarian regimes, it remains unclear why Brazilian authoritarianism, with a tradition at least 250 years old, is more situational than, for example, that of Spain, which is now undergoing a "democratic" renaissance.

Unquestionably, a great deal more work needs to be done on authoritarian systems, relating detailed empirical research to theoretical analysis. Not enough is understood about how economic modernization is managed by traditional institutions which, despite extensive social change, maintain a stratified access to the political process and concentration of power in the hands of the state. In particular, there is insufficient insight into the relationship of day to day decision making to the maintenance and continuity of the political order. For example, despite the fact that the general literature on Brazil is abundant and that in recent yers a number of studies have appered focusing on Brazilian authoritarianism and corporatism, detailed issue oriented case studies of policy and decision making are few.[7] Furthermore, for the most part, these studies do not explore the larger theoretical implications of their findings or place the issues they discuss in a developmental perspective. Consequently, comparability based on a common frame of reference is reduced, and theoretical implications must often be inferred.

Of the three recent major case study approaches, only one, for instance, that of Nathaniel Leff, makes an explicit attempt to provide a comprehensive theoretical explanation of the nature of the Brazilian decision making process.[8] His provocative review of economic decision making within four issue areas from 1947 to 1964 emphasizes executive discretion and autonomy in the policy process, and the powerlessness of traditional elites against the executive technocrats. He attributes the rational, independent role of the executive to a combination of clientelistic political organization and a political consensus akin to Rousseau's general will.[9] In his view, class and interest group analyses, which attribute considerable political power to economic groups, are inapplicable to the Brazilian situation.[10] In the absence of a powerful interest framework, the executive is apparently in a position to effect a number of rational, innovative policy decisions even when they are unpopular with particular economic and social sectors.

Unfortunately, although Leff's analysis offers some interesting insights into economic decision making for the 1947-1964 period, several weaknesses limit the general validity of its observations on the relationship of decision making to the social and political order. For one thing, President João Goulart (1961-1964) clearly did not fit the description of the powerful executive unhampered by social and political considerations in the formulation of policy. Second, Leff's description of the role of interest groups, while again occasionally insightful, misses the mark because Brazilian interest groups are not by any means without influence. Furthermore, as this study will show, under certain circumstances, they are powerful indeed.

The authors of the other two studies, Schneider on foreign policy making and Hirschman on socioeconomic policy affecting the Brazilian Northeast, concur in the assessment of a powerful Brazilian executive which plays a dominant role in the decision making process.[11] However, each in different ways paints a considerably more complex picture of that process. Schnedier, for example, while acknowledging the clearly elitist basis of foreign policy, alludes to extensive intramular struggles in the executive branch.[12] Furthermore, although he does not provide an explicit analysis of social structure and its impact on the conduct of foreign policy, he does affirm its importance in influencing the scope and direction of foreign policy decisions.[13] He relates the conduct of Brazilian foreign policy to the domestic economic and political situation and indicates how changes in the latter can affect Brazil's conduct in the international arena. Even nongovernmental groups whose interest in foreign affairs is sporadic and whose role is informal and ad hoc at best do occasionally influence foreign policy. Thus, in Schneider's view, the dominance of the executive and the weakness of organized interests is not imcompatible with bargaining and the formulation of political strategies. On the contrary, although the immediate policy arena may be restricted, successful domestic strategies underlie even though they do not control the conduct of an effective foreign policy.

Hirschman's account of how the Superintendency of the Northeast (SUDENE) was created likewise affirms the central role of the executive. Nevertheless, this crucial struggle over resources was "marked by bitter and protracted battles, unexpected switches, and narrow margins of victory rather than sudden unanimity."[14] In stressing the role of a wide range of interests in the policy process, Hirschman situates the powerful executive in a complex and interactive political framework. He observes that presidential interest is a determining factor in the successful passage of social legislation. However, traditional interests can and do affect policy outcome, especially during "democratic" periods when regional political elites can express themselves through Congress. He concludes that pragmatism and coalition building are an essential feature of the Brazilian policy process, and that the context within which an issue is discussed or implemented substantially affects the definition of the policy and its application.[15]

The different interpretations of the policy process, as defined in case study approaches by the three authors, owes a great deal to the distinct issue areas they address and the time frame within which the issues are considered. In contrast to the other two works, Hirschman's study analyzes a controversial issue whose importance is not only economic, but also social and political. This suggests that within a reasonably open political situation, when debate and organizational activity are permitted, specific traditional interests are more likely to express themselves on critical social issues which might affect their political status. Leff himself notes that the shift of emphasis to basic reforms in the early 1960s "contrasted with the previous concentration on economic development, without explicit focus on social and political changes."[16] Unfortunately, he does not examine the implications of this observation for his own analytical model of the Brazilian decision making process. When one considers the relative powerlessness of João Goulart in his struggle to effect policy changes it becomes clear that executive power is conditioned by social and political factors not discussed by Leff. In this sense, his analysis is incomplete.

In discussing social and foreign policy, Hirschman and Schneider fill some of the lacunae left by Leff, but likewise do not present us with a complete view of the political structure and its relationship to decision making in Brazil, in good part because such was not their intention. They too, therefore, leave conceptual gaps to be filled out by additional research and analysis of other issues. Not all issues, however, are equally useful for exploring the relationship between the policy process and the maintenance of the political order. Logically, the greatest yield will come from broad social issues that affect the definition of authority and the distribution of power in society.

THE CASE OF LAND REFORM

The controversy over land reform in Brazil during the early 1960s lends itself particularly well to a study of the relationship between the policy process and the development and preservation of the political system. As one of the most important issues of the time, land reform was widely debated over a period of years spanning two different regimes separated by a major political upheaval in 1964. In fact, the land reform controversy contributed importantly to the overthrow of President João Goulart and the establishment of the military regime which has since been in power.

The intensity of discussion and degree of political mobilization generated by land reform make it an ideal issue for exploring a series of important questions about the Brazilian authoritarian system. First, since land reform threatened a redistribution of property and power, the response of established elites can be viewed as a measure of the resilience of political system in coping with social change and demands for a more equitable distribution of resources. Second, a careful examination of the issue can help clarify which social groups determine the nature of the issues that can be raised for overt policy consideration, under what circumstances, and with what consequences. Third, this examination would indicate the terms on which powerful traditional elites accept social and economic change. Finally, this study should tell us something about the rules, customs, and style of a major political debate in a traditional authoritarian system.

The discussion of the policy struggle over land reform begins in chapter two with a review of the historical importance of the agrarian sector and the role played by the landed elites in the development and transformation of the Brazilian patrimonial state. The historical and institutional analysis is concluded with a close look at the social and political organization of the agrarian sector on the eve of the land reform debate and a clarification of the apparent as well as the more substantive stakes in the controversy. Chapter three examines the attempt to formulate agrarian policy from the perspective of the executive. Equally important, however, it uses this major redistributive issue to explore the developmental problems of the Brazilian presidency and to assess its impact on the political and institutional crisis which resulted in the fall of the Goulart administration. The next chapter, on the Congress, in addition to serving the same purpose, provides an opportunity to examine more closely the influence and impact of social and economic interest groups in an openly competitive political situation. It thus supplies means for evaluating the representativeness, responsiveness, and efficacy of Brazilian democracy. This theme is explored in somewhat greater detail in chapter four, which uses a content analysis of debates in the lower house of the Brazilian Congress to measure the relevance of party membership, state of origin, and ideological conviction in the positions adopted by Brazilian elected politicians in a formal policy setting. Finally, the last chapter assesses the nature and impact of the agrarian law and policy implemented by the military government and reviews the insights provided by this policy analysis into the nature of the Brazilian authoritarian state, its strengths and weaknesses, and its methods in coping with stress and change.

NOTES

1. Barrington Moore, Jr., Social Origins of Dictatorship and Democracy. Lord and Peasant in the Making of the Modern World (Boston: Beacon Press, 1966), especially ch. 9, "The Peasants and Revolution," pp. 453-483. See also Samuel P. Huntington, Political Order in Changing Societies (New Haven: Yale University Press, 1968) especially pp. 291-300, in ch. 5, "Revolution and the Political Order."

2. See especially Alfred Stepan, editor, Authoritarian Brazil. Origins, Policies, and Future (New Haven: Yale University Press, 1973). Philippe Schmitter's essay "The Portugalization of Brazil?" provides a particularly useful discussion of political continuity, and is complemented by Thomas S. Skidmore's "Politics and Economic Policy Making" in the same volume, especially pp. 31-43. See also Ronald M. Schneider, Brazil: Foreign Policy of a Future World Power (Boulder, Colorado: Westview Press, 1976), pp. 4-5, and Kenneth P. Erickson, The Brazilian Corporative State and Working Class Politics (Berkeley: University of California Press, 1977).

3. This argument is fully developed by Raymundo Faoro, Os Donos do Poder. A Formação do Patronato Político Brasileiro (Pôrto Alegre: Editôra Globo, 1958).

4. Current interest in this subject owes a great deal to the path breaking work of Juan J. Linz. Apart from his influential essay "An Authoritarian Regime: Spain" in Erik Allardt and Yrjo Littune, editors, Cleavages, Ideologies, and Party Systems (Helsinki, 1964), Linz's popular lectures at Columbia University gave much food for thought to future generations of scholars. On authoritarianism, generally, see also Samuel Huntington and Clement H. Moore, editors, Authoritarian Politics in Modern Society (New York: Basic Books, 1970).

5. Juan J. Linz, "The Future of an Authoritarian Situation," in Authoritarian Brazil, p. 236.

6. Ibid., pp. 235, 236.

7. Stepan, Authoritarian Brazil, Erickson, The Brazilian

Corporative State, Ronald M. Schneider, The Political System of Brazil: Emergence of a 'Modernizing' Authoritarian Regime, 1964-1970) (New York: Columbia University Press, 1971), Philippe C. Schmitter, Interest Conflict and Political Change in Brazil (Stanford, Cal., Stanford University Press, 1971) are major English language sources on the subject.

8. Nathaniel Leff, Economic Policy-Making and Development in Brazil, 1947-1964 (New York, Wiley, 1968).

9. Ibid., pp. 113-118.

10. Ibid., pp. 3-4, 179-181.

11. Schneider, Brazil. Foreign Policy of a Future World Power; Albert O. Hirschman, Journeys Toward Progress, (New York: Doubleday, 1965), ch. 1 "Brazil's Northeast," pp. 29-129.

12. Foreign Policy, p. 127.

13. Ibid., pp. 165-225.

14. Journeys Toward Progress, p. 57.

15. Ibid., p. 343.

16. Economic Policy Making, p. 168.

2. Land, Tradition, and the Socio-Political Order

Since its independence in 1821, Brazil has experienced several major changes of regime, An extended period of stable monarchical rule, the Empire, gave way in 1889 to a highly decentralized, federated republic ruled by state oligarchies. The First, or Old Republic was abolished in 1930 by a revolution which ushered in a fifteen year dictatorship by Getúlio Vargas. From 1945 to 1964, a crisis ridden Second Republic reintroduced decentralized and competitive politics within a liberal democratic framework. Since 1964, Brazil has been ruled by an overtly authoritarian and politically conservative military regime.

At first glance, the changes of regime since 1930 in particular invite speculation that they reflect fundamental alterations of the social and economic relationships resulting from rapid modernization. Yet, in fact, Brazil's industrial and economic growth have been achieved not at the expense of, but within a traditional institutional context. Under the impact of industralization and modernization, systems of direct, reciprocal social relations and strong, affective personal ties have not been transformed into impersonal, instrumental relations and interest oriented class politics. Instead, quasi-familial ties of patronage, clientelism, and mutual obligation have endured and served as the social basis of economic transformation.[1] Recurrent political instability, while symptomatic of unresolved contradictions in the political order, should not distract our attention from the fact that the Brazilian traditional order has thus far ably survived the crises of modernization and will probably continue to do so.

The Brazilian experience of modernization in an authoritarian framework owes its success to the sustained evolution of a centralized patrimonial state exercising its authority through a status bureaucracy while conciliating powerful landholding and urban economic interests. Traditionally, the legitimacy of the state's authority has rested on its performing a guardian role for the society. Less a voice of the people than an interpreter of their well-being, the state assumed the role of mediator and impartial judge, not swayed by partisan interests, and concerned only for the general good of the whole society. At the time of the Empire, this role became explicitly formalized as the poder moderador (moderating power) and officially ascribed to the emperor. The society he ruled was perceived to consist of noncompeting segments whose special needs and contributions were to be coordinated into a harmonious whole in which selfish interests would be constrained by the benevolent and impartial state.

As economic modernization began to transform Brazilian society, the patrimonial bureaucratic state faced the immediate and continuous challenge of successfully altering the traditional basis of its economy and incorporating new social and economic sectors into the political order in such a way as neither to threaten its elitist orientation nor erode its corporatist and statist ethic of legitimacy. To a considerable extent, its ability to accomplish this end can be ascribed to the social control exercised over vast rural areas by a stable and powerful agrarian sector. Once the predominent basis of Brazil's mercantilist economy, the traditionally organized agrarian sector preserved its continuity and power against new economic and political contenders by its ability to define the limits of acceptable change. In alliance with military and ecclesiastical power, the landed elite yielded to necessary modernization and social change in the urban areas (since it did not immediately threaten their social control in the rural area), but rose to overthrow any attempted move to restructure the traditional patrimonial order.

As Raymundo Faoro indicates, the basic features of the elitist and status based Brazilian political order have survived into the modern era.

> This autonomous minority power, neither controlled nor limited by the popular will, exercises through the bureaucrat, militaryman, and clergyman the political patronate that influences and directs social movements. . . . Its dominion is assured by the fundamental regulation of the economy, [a prerogative]. . . secured by the patrimonial regime and perpetuated in state capitalism. Political office holders, even when selected by a majority in elections or assemblies, do not succeed in surmounting this tutelary shield, but rather, accommodate to it, delighting in its privileges and attempting to perpetuate themselves [in power] . . . through the enslavement of electoral clienteles.[2]

Periodically, the basic features of this system have been obscured by an overlay of liberal democracy. The First and Second Republics both seemed to herald a new era of representative, if not precisely democratic government. However, in each case, the authoritarian state reasserted itself after an interval, dispensing with the electoral game and revealing the highly centralized elitist arrangements at its core.

AGRARIAN SOCIETY AND BUREAUCRATIC PATRIMONIAL STATE

Colony and Empire

During the colonial period, from the early sixteenth century until 1808 when King João VI moved the Portuguese court to Brazil in advance of the Napoleonic invasion, the colony's importance to the mother country was based on extractive enterprises, both agricultural and mineral, entrusted to loyal followers. The royal land grant system was based on a 1375 Portuguese law, by which the king parcelled out *sesmarias*, individual grants of a size that could be cultivated by one individual.[3] Failure to cultivate property could result in the expropriation and redistribution of the land. The purpose of the legislation was both to increase agricultural productivity and to prevent any further accretion in the power of the aristocracy, whose influence the crown was whittling away with the support of urban commerical groups and a newly powerful state bureaucracy.

In the new world, the social and economic impact of the *sesmarias* was quite the contrary of that intended. The great distance between the colony and mother country, and the enormous expanse of the new territory made efficient administration and central control difficult. More important still was the influence of demographic factors on the pattern of settlement and land use. Portugal's limited ability to send large numbers of settlers meant that except for small and scattered populations of natives, the vast new territory, covering almost half of South America, was largely unpopulated. The existence of a sparse population combined with a great abundance of land did little to encourage the formation of a farmer class. Instead, huge estates controlled by a small planter elite came into being. In the absence of a local labor force, the land was worked by slaves brought from Africa. Brazil thus became a land of great commercial plantations characterized by a highly stratified pyramidal society, in which a large peasant-slave population supported a privileged aristocracy at its apex.

Nevertheless, as Warren Dean observes, from a political standpoint the Brazilian sesmaria system "was entirely functional from the perspective of the Portuguese Crown. The owners of the latifundia [were]. . . in normal times willingly subservient to imperial interests. They sent Lisbon their sugar and hides . . . [and] remained dependent on Portuguese merchants for credit and slaves." In the scramble for preferential treatment from the mother country, "the Brazilian planters were kept busy plotting against each other rather than the Crown."[4]

In 1821, after the imperial court returned to Portugal, Brazil declared its independence. But, in proclaiming the Empire, it retained the monarchical form of government and continued to be ruled by members of the same royal family. Unlike the Spanish colonies, Brazil did not, therefore, experience a major disruption in its political development at the time of independence. Institutional arrangements and the relationship of the emperor to his subjects remained largely unaltered. The emperor was vested with the poder moderador, an arbitral function, based on an implicit plebiscitary consensus to conciliate conflict and impose unity.[5] In the exercise of his powers, he continued to benefit from intra-elite strife and governed with the aid of a complex and powerful bureaucracy. The imperial bureaucracy, a political legacy of the mother country, enabled the emperor to avoid exclusive dependence on the landed elite by relying on a functionary, or bureaucratic nobility, which he could name and remove at will.

The status bureaucracy functioned as an organ of social control, coopting politically ambitious individuals and socializing them into its comfortable and prestigious ranks. In this sense, the Brazilian Empire could be compared to other agrarian bureaucratic empires, of which the Chinese serves as a good example.[6] Eisenstadt observes that rulers of such empires had to find allies "among the groups and strata whose interests were opposed to those of the more traditional and aristocratic groups, and who could benefit from their weakening and from the establishment of a more unified policy." Urban centers, with their populations of varied economic, cultural, and professional groups, were particularly useful sources of such allies, who were recruited not on the basis of kinship or territorial origin, but of "skill, wealth, achievement, or political loyalty to the rulers."[7] By this means, the Brazilian emperor was able to exercise considerable power in the face of traditional agrarian opposition to the central control of the state.

Although their direct influence on national policy was limited, the power of the landed elite was not negligible. The very vastness of Brazil and the difficulties of communication afforded the landowners considerable local social hegemony and economic autonomy. But even so, on the local level, the landowners' power was qualified in a number of respects. Both appointive and electoral systems worked to imperial benefit. For example, until the abolition of the monarchy in 1889 when many powers were decentralized to the states, the police system was centralized. The imperial government appointed district police delegates nominated by the imperial chief of police, who, in turn, was appointed by the emperor.[8] The electoral system, besides functioning to ratify appointments made from the top, was skewed to urban areas, which contained a disproportionate number of eligible (i.e., literate and propertied) voters. Thus, the central government skillfully exploited a variety of control mechanisms at its disposal.

The Old Republic

The establishment of a republic following the military overthrow of the Empire in 1889 was the first of two major experiences in the decentralization of the authoritarian Brazilian state. Since the demise of the monarchy was linked to the rise of urban republican sentiments that had been responsible for the abolition of slavery, the change of regime might have seemed at the outset to be inimical to agrarian interests. Yet, in fact, the contrary was true. The extreme decentralization of government under the Old Republic contributed to the preemienence of regional and state interests and of local power. At this time of the "politics of the governors," national affairs, which included the elections of the president, were settled by a process of adjustment and compromise among state oligarchies. Among these, the most powerful were those of São Paulo and Minas Gerais, which took turns in controlling the presidency in an arrangement called "coffee and milk" for the two states' principal products, coffee and livestock. A network of _coroneis_, by and large local _fazendeiros_ (landowners), supported the oligarchic political machines and supplied them with votes in return for public power.[9] The _coronel_, essentially a traditional political boss, controlled a clan which competed with other clans for local control. The _coroneis_ served as links in a chain of reciprocal relations between the _municípios_ (local districts) and state oligarchies, of which the most powerful _coroneis_ were members. The entire rural political system was based on the manipulation of a submissive and dependent rural working population by the large proprietors.

Despite the abolition of slavery in 1888, the social and economic power of landowners did not suffer from the change of regime. The commercial exploitation of agriculture for export purposes continued to be basis of the economy, and rural labor, although freed, remained exploited and dependent. Paid labor had already begun to replace the slave system after a ban on slave trading in 1850. From then until emancipation, the planter class had the opportunity to work out new dependency relations with its labor force.[10] The continued control of large property owners was insured by the chronic exploitation and indebtedness of the laborers and a web of social and political obligations of small owners, sharecroppers, and hired labor to large landowners.

It is from this era of the "politics of the governors" that the stereotype of the all powerful landowner derives. Indeed, during the Old Republic, the power of the planter class to organize the populations dependent on it into efficient political machines was impressive, but it was not unlimited. The countervailing power of the centralized and urban based bureaucracies had been curtailed but not abolished. As Brazil began the process of industrialization, these support sectors of the centralized state together with modernizing elements of the military reasserted themselves forcefully.

The Vargas Dictatorship

The revolution of 1930, which ended the Old Republic, was ushered in by a revolt of young army lieutenants and precipitated by a dispute over the presidential elections of that year.[11] Its importance, however, extended well beyond this specific event. Reflecting the turbulence of the initial phase of modernization, it served as the vehicle for the entry of the middle class into the political arena and set the stage for the political incorporation of urban labor as well.

However, the demise of the Old Republic did not give way, as the middle class had hoped, to a liberal democracy. Instead, the modern industrial era was begun under the auspices of the fifteen year dictatorship of the former governor of Rio Grande do Sul and leader of the insurrection, Getúlio Vargas. In his study of the Vargas regime, Robert Levine notes the irony of the middle class' situation when he observes that the very acts of the government in 1934 and 1935 to restore democratic procedures through free elections threatened to return state control to the rural oligarchies, which, through alliances with local bosses, or coroneis, generally controlled local voting.[12]

In the face of these circumstances, urban middle class opposition to strongman rule eventually turned to accommodation with what it considered the lesser of two evils.

Further incentive for collaboration was provided by what Hélio Jaguaribe has called the "Cartorial State," a system in which the state exercised a policy of patronage by increasing the number of public service posts to secure political support in return for government employment.[13] Lured by the promise of status and security, the middle class was coopted into implicit collaboration with the corporatist strategy to maintain traditional statist authority, and "showed itself . . . neither inclined nor able to use the apparatus of government to bring about a complete transformation of the country's economic and social structure."[14] In Jaguaribe's scheme, the expanded patronage role of the state was an easy alternative to a more economically rational policy of systematic industrialization. Such a policy might have more effectively resolved the economic needs of the middle class while contributing toward its independent political development. Yet, in fact, it was this latter consideration that made "cartorialism" an entirely rational strategy for a modernizing traditional authoritarian order whose first priority was self preservation. The Vargas years may have been erratic from the viewpoint of a planned industrial development strategy. But, in retrospect, they must be judged as a necessary exercise in institution building to bridge the transition between an agrarian patrimonial past and an industrial future presided over by a modern authoritarian state.

An important aspect of this effort was the formalization of the relationship of society to state along corporatist lines. The supremacy of the state as a disinterested arbiter of conflicting interests and as an expression of the general will of all the people was reaffirmed. But where little grass roots associational activity had existed before, Vargas promoted the establishment of an official syndical interest structure, sponsored and regulated by the state.[16] By this means, the previously implicit notions of the relationship of concrete socioeconomic interests to the moderating power of the state were explicitly defined in a legal framework whose dimensions and rationale, while native in origin, resembled the efforts of European fascist regimes during that same inter-war period.

According to the dictates of the Consolidated Labor Code of 1943, the corporatist interest structure was to be organized into syndicates that were to function as exclusive representatives of their members' interests to the state.[17] The federated interest structure essentially followed the political organization of the nation. Thus, in the industrial and commerical sectors, where early syndicalization efforts made greatest headway, separate employer and employee syndicates were organized for each occupation at the <u>município</u> level. Local organizations were then grouped into state federations which, in turn, were united into national confederations. By means of this device, Vargas was able to create an organized national labor movement where virtually none had existed before. More important still from the perspective of statist development, that movement was malleable and dependent, and constituted a political tool in the hands of the government.

From the perspective of the agrarian elite, the Vargas years constituted the first phase of a long term process which, while subordinating the rural power structure to the state, assured its continued viability and reaffirmed its importance in the political order. In broad lines, the new centralized structure of the _Estado Nôvo_ resembled that which had existed under the Empire. The national bureaucracies regained their strength through central coordination, and the executive drew its major support from urban commercial and professional groups, as well as from the military and the emerging industrial and organized labor groups flourishing under government tutelage.

State governments were stripped of the military and economic prerogatives they had enjoyed under the Old Republic, but the rural power structure was not so much humbled as reincorporated by the central government. Vargas shrewdly perceived the utility of working with rather than against the still powerful _coroneis_. In an accommodation with the new regime, the _fazendeiros_ looked for continued access to federal power and patronage and noninterference in the rural social structure. Vargas, in turn, needed at least the acquiescence of the agricultural elite to pursue his economic plans, a major aspect of which required financing industrialization with agricultural, and particularly coffee profits.[18] In addition, the solid traditional political control of rural areas could contribute to general political stability during a turbulent period of rapid urbanization. For these reasons, Vargas willingly refrained from disturbing the traditional social organization of rural areas and the local control of the landed elite. Instead, his agrarian policies emphasized encouragement of modern methods of agricultural production, without making them mandatory. To this end, he created a separate Ministry of Agriculture and a number of federal commodity institutes, and promoted crop diversification and domestic consumption.[19]

But although it was not affected as much as the urban sector, agriculture was not entirely omitted from syndical organization. On October 24, 1945, Vargas signed the enabling regulations for organizing agriculture.[20] Decree law 8127 mandated the establishment of an official representational structure for the rural sector and brought into being the Brazilian Rural Confederation (CRB). Like other confederations, the CRB consisted of local "associations," grouped into state federations. However, in contrast to urban syndical organization, it did not stipulate the creation of separate organizations for employers and employees. In other words, the state effectively refrained from challenging the rural oligarchy's control of its labor force, as well as of renters and small property owners traditionally under its domination. Rural labor expert Arno Schilling has observed that this interpretation of the criteria for membership in the CRB was prompted by a concern on the part of the government that an incipient unionization movement in the countryside might fragment the political control of the latifundium.[21] For the time being, the government preferred to exercise indirect control through its influence with the agricultural elite.

The concentration on urban economic development and the absence of compelling political and economic incentives to alter traditional land tenure and productive arrangements temporarily shielded the agricultural sector from the modernizing pressures transforming the urban economy. But the countryside could not withstand these pressures indefinitely. The intermittent polemics over the agrarian problem during the post World War II period finally culminated in the land reform crisis which is the focus of this study.

The Second Republic

Vargas stepped down from power in 1945 in the face of widespread public demand for an end to arbitrary rule.[22] The new constitution of 1945 formally established a liberal democracy with a federated republican political system. However, much like the revolution of 1930, the change of regime produced no major alteration either in the role of the state, or the social and economic structure supporting it.

Superficially, the multiparty electoral system that functioned from 1946 to 1964 and the expansion of suffrage to all literate persons over eighteen appeared to be a genuine response to the demand for a democratization of the decision making process.[23] In fact, it neither rationalized nor democratized that process. The three major political parties that emerged in 1945 were firmly rooted in the manipulative and elitist politics of the preceding era. Indeed, two of them, the Social Democratic Party (PSD), and the Brazilian Labor Party (PTB), were created by Vargas himself. The PSD, frequently referred to as the party of the coroneis, consisted largely of the state party machines that dominated the politics of the First Republic. The PTB, referred to as the party of *pelegos* (government flunkeys)[24] by its detractors, originated in the labor movement organized by Vargas during the *Estado Nôvo* to serve as his personal machine for controlling labor. Finally, the National Democratic Union (UDN), the party of liberal intellectuals, or *bachareis*, united an assortment of anti-Vargas groups active in promoting a change of regime. Reflecting their origin, the primary distinction among the parties remained their historical attitude toward Getúlio. The absence of issue orientation in the parties was emphasized by their pragmatic and opportunistic behavior, reflected in high levels of factionalism and coalitions of a purely instrumental nature linking unlikely allies in an inconsistent pattern from state to state and from state to federal level.

Party organization was clientelistic and party loyalties were established principally on the basis of personal ties. *Coronelism* persisted in the countryside, and in the cities the *cabo eleitoral* (political boss) or *político de clientela* (clientele politician) emerged as his urban counterparts.[25] The clientelistic basis of party politics went hand in hand with the Cartorial State, delivering patronage in return for promises of political support.

Not all elections, however, lent themselves equally well to direct, personal, clientelistic manipulation, be it by urban, or even rural political bosses. In particular, clientelistic control tended to be reduced in urban areas where large electorates reflected a higher rate of literacy, which was a requirement for voting. It was also modified to the extent that a specific election was to be decided by a majority vote as opposed to proportional representation, and in elections whose the geographic scope encompassed large political units. These conditions especially prevailed in the elections for president and state governors.

But a lesser control by political machines did not by any means turn elections into vehicles of grass roots interests and issues.[26] On the contrary, the conduct of majority elections played a companion role to that of clientelism in blurring issues and suppressing consciousness of class interests. Since electoral options in rural areas were already monopolized by rural party bosses, political newcomers settled on a populist antiestablishment style.[27] Paternalistic in overtones, like clientelism, populism attracted newly emerging urban constituencies by appealing to their inarticulate discontent and anomic frustrations. Populist politicians amassed large followings not by organizing around distinct issues or concrete social programs but through charisma and demagoguery. They fashioned vague promises of nationalist reforms or spiritual rejuvenation which appealed indiscriminately to a wide social spectrum, and produced the electoral majorities they needed to launch and sustain them in power.

Thus, the major political phenomena of Brazilian electoral politics, clientelism, populism, and coronelismo, were modalities of an authoritarian corporatist system and served as elite strategies in the ever-expanding competition for power, position, and status. What changed in the course of electoral expansion and urbanization was not so much the basic character and purpose of the leadership, but rather, the strategies used to achieve the leadership's aims within the existing framework.

The strategy of accommodating demands from the middle class and urban labor for greater participation by establishing a competitive but still elite manipulated electoral system ultimately proved to be a problematic and short term solution. During the 1945-1964 democratic interlude, and particularly starting with the second (this time elected) Vargas presidency (1951-1954) Brazil was progressing from spontaneous industrialization by import substitution to a phase of planned economic development concentrating on establishing a solid domestic industrial base.[28] The accomplishment of this task would ultimately require modernizing more then just the economy, including the traditional agrarian section. It also required the revamping of elitist political institutions to reflect the exigencies of popular participation. The most sensitive problem, from this perspective, was the development of a political framework capable of absorbing newly mobilized social sectors without endangering the security and stability of the traditional political order which was presiding over the process of economic transformation.

The electoral system did indeed reach out to erstwhile unpoliticized populations, and in some sense might have been perceived as an adjunct aggregative mechanism complementing the cartorial bureaucracy. But its nature and functioning aggravated political instability instead of mitigating it. Apart from sacrificing issue and interest oriented political discussion to vague demagogic populist appeals and clientelistic manipulation, it introduced and progressively reinforced a serious contradition between the process by which political leadership was brought to power and the means by which it could exercise that power. Effective decision making still had to be based on the acquiescence of patrimonial and corporatist sources of authority, consisting of conservative, traditional elites. The road to power, on the other hand, increasingly lay in the populist expolitation of an electorate expanding rapidly because of population growth, increasing literacy, and a heightened political consciousness among both urban and rural masses.

These circumstances imposed an especially heavy burden on the nation's political leadership, and particularly the president, in their efforts to produce and effect a coherent developmental strategy. Executive pursuit of developmental goals required striking a balance between their acceptability to traditional elites and international lending institutions, and their nationalist and radically reformist appeal to the masses. The difficulty of this task is underscored by the fact that during the democratic interval, only one president, Juscelino Kubitschek (1956-1961), succeeded in making this formula work. He brilliantly exploited an era of dynamic growth through import substitution measures that projected an image of Brazil as a successful model of democratic modernization for Latin America. It was widely assumed that Brazil had discovered the ideal formula for pursuing populist political strategies and economic development while maintaining the good will and even support of the patrimonial elites. In fact, Juscelino's success lay in exploiting a strategy not of change, but of postponement. In a move reminiscent of Vargas, the problem of the traditional agrarian structure was deferred by a tactical compromise with the landed elite to refrain from altering rural relations. Instead, Juscelino concentrated in his "Target Program" on relatively "safe" economic policy making which promoted urban industrial growth.

However, Juscelino's ability to postpone confrontation with the agrarian issue made his presidency uniquely stable and successful. The political and constitutional crises of the second Vargas presidency, and of the Jânio Quadros and João (Jango) Goulart administrations reflected far more accurately the critical stresses and contradictions between the needs of modernization and the requirements of authority and stability inherent in the traditional Brazilian order. After unsuccessfully grappling with the contradictions of instituting change within a basically conservative and traditional structure allied to a populist mobilizing system, Vargas committed suicide in office in August 1954; UDN-supported Quadros, who came to power with a landslide vote and a promise to sweep the government clean,[29] resigned after seven months in office in August 1961; and finally, in attempting to pass basic structural reforms, including a major land reform, Vargas' protege Goulart was deposed by a military/civilian coup which simultaneously terminated the democratic interlude.

RURAL MOBILIZATION AND LAND REFORM

The Brazilian democratic experiment ended in the midst of a heated debate over land reform that reflected the culmination of a sociopolitical crisis long in the making. Brazil's political leadership had deliberately postponed the problems of integrating the agrarian sector into the modern economy and incorporating the rural lower class into the political process. In so doing, it purchased some time and illusory stability to undergo industrialization. But in the long run, it was impossible to isolate the countryside from the impact of economic and political changes originating in urban areas or from nationalist and exogenous reformist ideologies. Moreover, the economic imperative to integrate the old plantations into a modern framework coincided with increased rural unrest and mounting efforts by leftist urban organizers to politicize and mobilize the *camponeses*.*

Viewed against the background of the political events of the time, the agrarian issue reflected the convergence and mutual reinforcement of three major issues: 1) the strain between the electoral and authority systems; 2) the threat which social and political mobilization (both urban and rural) posed to the control mechanisms of the patrimonial system; and 3) the dilemma of how to modernize and rationalize an inefficient and exploitative agricultural sector and integrate it into the rest of the economy with a minimum of political disruption.

The Land Reform Issue

By the early 1960s, a sharp increase in rural unrest lent new urgency to a long-standing concern

*No single English word fully corresponds to the meaning of *camponês*. It can mean peasant, countryman, farmer, cottager, all denoting different types of agricultural experience. For this reason, the Portuguese word is used throughout the text, in preference to "peasant."

over the backward state of Brazilian agriculture. Among traditional landowners and conservative allies opposition to change in rural areas persisted. But the political and economic exigencies resulting from several decades of modernization determined that the articulation of a coherent agrarian policy could no longer be postponed. Economic disparities between the modern industrial sector and the traditional agrarian sector were becoming increasingly dysfunctional. Additional pressure for change came from leftist populist politicians who argued for a comprehensive land reform law that would promote social and economic justice in the countryside.

Ample evidence seemed to support their allegations of the gravity of the rural crisis. The distribution of property and the living and working conditions of rural labor were indicative of systematic exploitation and an extreme inequality of resources. According to a 1965 cadastral survey, 50 percent of all farm land (176,175,062 hectares)* was owned by 1.5 percent of all property owners. The great majority of farm owners, or 63 percent, owned only 6.3 percent of all farm land (11,537,812 hectares), and 44.8 percent of all individually held properties were 10 hectares (24.7 acres) or less. Since twenty hectares was considered the minimum amount of land needed to support a farming family, these figures indicated the existence of a large number of minifundia, or noneconomic size plots.[30]

This extreme inequality of land ownership cannot be explained merely by reference to Brazil's large

---

* One hectare equals 2.47 acres.

scale commercial agriculture. Commercial exploitation of land for the production and exportation of coffee, sugar, cotton, livestock, etc., figured prominently in the rural economy, and historically constituted the basis of Brazil's export earnings. But a full seventy-six percent of all farm properties were officially classified as latifundia, i.e., large unproductive or only partially productive estates. Likewise, the obvious pressure on land indicated by the number of minifundia and latifundia should not be construed to mean that Brazil had no reserves of unoccupied land. A considerable investment in extensive infrastructural development could transform the vast stretches of virgin territory into farm land. However, where the population was most dense, the quality of land good, and communication and transportation reasonably developed, the conditions of land ownership were highly unequal and exploitative.

The pattern of land tenure in Brazil and the role it played in the widespread unrest of the early 1960s was not atypical of Latin America in general. Nor did it constitute the most extreme case of maldistribution. Of seven Latin American countries studied by the Interamerican Committee for Agricultural Development (CIDA) in the early 1960s, Brazil had neither the most unequal land distribution, nor the largest percentage of minifundia or latifundia (see table 2-1). For example, at that time, the concentration of farm land in the hands of few owners was far greater in both Chile and Peru, and the problem of minifundia was more accentuated in Guatemala, Peru, and Ecuador.

But although Brazil's land distribution was not

the worst in Latin America, the rural conditions and tenancy arrangements were deplorable by any standard.[31] In 1963 over half of Brazil's population of 70,967,000, or 39,031,850 people, lived in rural areas.[32] Of the total employable rural population, estimated at about 25,000,000, there were almost five million unemployed rural workers. Furthermore, a vast majority of those fortunate enough to find work did not enjoy a decent standard of living. Fully half of all rural employed persons were salaried workers, sharecroppers, or renters. CIDA's Brazilian report noted that whereas in 1960 the rural population constituted 55 percent of the national total, it earned only 28 percent of the national income.[33] Debt peonage and long hours of exploited labor placed the work force at the political and economic mercies of absentee landlords. The physical and social consequences of these conditions were reflected in malnutrition, chronic health problems, high infant mortality, and a rural illiteracy rate of 90 percent, as compared to under 40 percent in urban areas.

Such conditions obviously could not result in maximum efficiency in the use of land or labor, not to speak of converting impoverished farmers into active participants of the consumer economy. Economists were becoming concerned that agriculture might constitute a stumbling block to continued economic expansion. Eventually, "industry is hampered by the low level of effective demand created by low rural incomes at the same time that high prices for agricultural raw materials and for wage goods contribute to high prices for industrial products."[34] To increase food production for internal markets and to expand the domestic market, the traditional rural

Table 2-1

RELATIVE NUMBER AND AREA OF FARM UNITS BY SIZE OF GROUP IN CIDA STUDY COUNTRIES (PERCENTAGE OF COUNTRY TOTAL IN EACH SIZE CLASS)

	Sub-family	Family	Medium multi-family	Large multi-family
Argentina				
number farm units	43.2	48.7	7.3	0.8
area in farms	3.4	44.7	15.0	36.9
Brazil				
number farm units	22.5	39.1	33.7	4.7
area in farms	0.5	6.0	34.0	59.5
Chile				
number farm units	36.9	40.0	16.2	6.9
area in farms	0.2	7.1	11.4	81.3
Colombia				
number farm units	64.0	30.2	4.5	1.3
area in farms	4.9	22.3	23.3	49.5
Ecuador				
number farm units	89.9	8.0	1.7	0.4
area in farms	16.6	19.0	19.3	45.1
Guatemala				
number farm units	88.4	9.5	2.0	0.1
area in farms	14.3	13.4	31.5	40.8
Peru				
number farm units	88.0	8.5	2.4	1.1
area in farms	7.4	4.5	5.7	82.4

Source: Solon L. Barraclough and Arthur L. Domike, "Agrarian Structure in Seven Latin American Countries," Land Economics 4(1966): 391-424 (© 1966 by the Board of Regents of the University of Wisconsin System), 48.

order would have to be transformed through reform and investment policies.

The argument for a review of agricultural policy acquired particular urgency under the pressure of social unrest in the countryside. By the late 1950s, rural malaise was reflected in land invasions and frequent outbreaks of violence between _fazendeiros_ and _camponeses_, especially in the Northeast and in the states of Minas Gerais and Rio de Janeiro. The concern of conservative elites over the revolutionary potential of these disturbances was intensified by pressures from outside the country. The recent Cuban revolution and land reform served as fresh reminders of the revolutionary potential of peasants and workers. In addition, responding to a similar concern, the Alliance for Progress inaugurated by President John F. Kennedy attempted to coax Latin American governments to enact agrarian reforms laws as a condition of receiving aid.[35]

It seemed, then, that for a variety of reasons -- social justice, defensive strategy against potential revolution, international pressure, and continued need for economic development -- a modernizing agrarian policy was not merely advisable, but imperative. However, the economic modernization of agricultural posed a major dilemma. Since the social organization of agriculture constituted the backbone of the Brazilian traditional political order, a modernizing policy implied the modernization of the patrimonial state itself. This required, among other far reaching changes, the orderly incorporation of an increasingly restive rural work force into the political process under circumstances which the planter class and other conservative elites considered to be especially adverse.[36]

Earlier, the political incorporation of the middle class and urban working class had been accomplished by the revolution of 1930 and the revival of the authoritarian patrimonial state by Getúlio Vargas.

The social and political organization of urban workers by the state prevented the development of the labor movement into an autonomous political force.[37] Moreover, during this early phase of industrial transformation, the cooperation of the traditional agrarian sector provided an important measure of stability and continuity. Now, agriculture itself was to be transformed and its social relations reorganized. Yet, the rural oligarchy's ability to define in its own favor the terms of lower class incorporation was compromised from 1945 to 1964 by the existence of a competitive, populist democratic system. The very functioning of that system tended to increase rural mobilization and introduced into the countryside radical ideologies challenging the hegemony of the landed elite. These circumstances seemed to confirm the fears of landowners and other conservative elites that at the heart of rational economic arguments for agrarian reform lay a direct threat to the existing political order and the traditional distribution of power and status.

Rural Organization: The Struggle for Control

Brazil had a long history of rural unrest, but the increase in rural tensions at this time was especially threatening. It occurred in conjunction with intensive organizational activity in the countryside. Unlike the secondary and tertiary sectors, the agrarian sector had escaped the full impact of Vargas' corporatist syndicalization effort during the *Estado Nôvo*.[38] Instead of creating separate employers' and employees' organizations, Vargas established a single rural confederation. Rural unionization remained illegal and rural salaried workers, small owners, renters, and sharecroppers remained under the unchallenged control of the large planters. Before the late 1950s only the Brazilian Communist Party attempted to organize rural labor by establishing a network of Ligas Camponesas -- not to be confused with the ligas later associated with Francisco Julião. Never numerous or strong, the communist Ligas foundered after the communist party was again declared illegal in 1947 following two years of public activity.

Organizational activity among the camponeses re-emerged in the mid fifties in the most depressed of Brazil's rural areas, the Northeast. With the assistance of ex-communist party member José dos Prazeres, the camponeses of the Galiléia sugar plantation organized the Agricultural Society of Planters and Cattle Ranchers of Pernambuco, (SAPP).[39] SAPP members quickly realized that the survival of the organization in the face of fazendeiro persecution would depend on securing political protection. Prazeres succeeded in getting the support of various political figures, including that of an ambitious young lawyer and Brazilian Socialist Party member, Francisco Julião de Paula. In little time, Julião became honorary president of what soon grew to be a network of ligas camponesas, as they were called by the latifundists "in an attempt to confuse them with the Liga of Iputinga and other defunct Communist peasant leagues."[40] The ligas continued to prosper and extend their network throughout the Northeast. Their activities received special impetus after reformist Cid Sampaio became governor of Pernambuco in 1959 and sanctioned the forced land distribution carried out by the ligas earlier.[41]

As talk of agrarian reform became widespread and the political climate for populist mobilization became more favorable, other agrarian organizations began to function. Among the more important were ULTAB, the Union of Agricultural Laborers and Workers of Brazil, originally created by the communist party in 1957, and MASTER, the Movement of Landless Associations, organized by Jango's brother-in-law, Leonel Brizola, in Rio Grande do Sul. Reformist Catholic clerics also joined the organizational effort, to the chagrin of their conservative brothers. Fathers Melo and Crespo sought to counter the influence of the "godless" ligas by setting up church sponsored unions in Pernambuco and Father Lagé's Radical Catholic Popular Action and Bishop Eugênio Sales' camponês unions appeared in various parts of the Northeast.[42] Rio Grande do Sul also boasted a flourishing church organized rural labor movement under the guidance of Bishop Dom Vicente Scherer. Even the Ministry of Labor, despite the absence of legislation legalizing rural unionization, supported camponês organization in the Northeast.

By the close of 1961 these organizational efforts seemed to be bearing fruit. According to liga camponesa and ULTAB estimates, their combined membership totalled approximately 550,000 persons.[43] The ULTAB estimate of 500,000 members may well have been inflated. But even if it possessed no more than the 200,000 individuals reported by Mary Wilkie,[44] when added to the ligas' 50,000 and the Catholic church's 45,000 in the Northeast and Rio Grande do Sul,[45] the rural labor movement demonstrated impressive growth where virtually no organization at all had existed as little as five years earlier. The first National

Conference of Farm Workers held in Belo Horizonte in November 1961 assembled 1,400 delegates and over 2,000 other participants who endorsed Julião's call for a radical land reform.[46]

It was against this background that the Goulart administration began to press for land reform and actively and officially supported the rural labor movement. On March 2, 1963 the president signed into law the Rural Worker bill introduced two years earlier by Deputy Fernando Ferrari.[47] The law legalized rural unionization for the first time and mandated the establishment of separate rural confederations for agricultural employers and employees. It designanated as rural "employees" all persons who worked for a rural employer in exchange for money or payment in kind. A rural "employer" was defined as an individual or corporation, whether property owner or not, who pursued economic activity in the countryside.[48]

Although the law was clearly a milestone in extending basic rights to rural workers, its reformist implications were somewhat ambiguous. By legalizing rural unions and providing rural workers with a separate confederation, it legitimized and lent special significance to the unauthorized but widespread rural mobilization of the last few years. Also, it provided the government with an official role and stake in the organizational effort. However, because it uncritically applied urban syndical legislation to rural areas, the law's reformist potential was suspect. By applying the simple urban legal dichotomy between workers and employers to the countryside, the law failed to recognize the diversity and complexity of agrarian economic relations. Specifically, it failed to recognize small property and minifundia owners, renters, and sharecroppers as distinct groups with unique problems and interests. Commenting on their perception of agrarian problems, Adolpho Puggina observed:

> The owner of a small property, sharecropper, and renter, are as interested in agrarian reform as are salaried rural workers, and if organized into their own unions would constitute a powerful force that could not only make demands, but also, and principally, offer invaluable collaboration with the authorities in the execution of an agrarian reform.[49]

Since these groups were not legally recognized as "employees" they automatically fell into the legal category of "employers" and therefore under the control of the large landowners.

In this context, the complacency with which large landowners initially regarded the introduction of the bill in Congress is understandable.[50] Apart from their expecting minimal enforcement of the law, they perceived that it allowed them to retain control over a considerable part of the rural occupational population. As the breakdown of the Brazilian rural occupational structure in table 2-2 indicates, salaried workers constituted 33.3 percent of economically active individuals in rural areas. Since medium to large landowners, that is, those capable of hiring workers, constituted 11 percent of the economically active rural population, the large landowners retained effective control of the remaining 55.6 percent, or 9,007,200 people and their dependent families. But João Goulart soon demonstrated that an apparently innocuous law could become a threatening instrument in the hands of even a weak president determined to generate new sources of political support.[51] The complacency of the landowners

Table 2-2

RURAL OCCUPATIONAL STRUCTURE, 1965

Category	Number	Percent
Owners with employees...........	1,783,832	11.0
Owners without employees.........	7,441,868	45.9
Renters.........................	220,000	1.4
Sharecroppers...................	1,358,000	8.4
Salaried workers................	5,396,300	33.3
Total.....................	16,200,000	100.0

Source: Estrutura Agrária Brasileira, and Chacel, p.114.

was effectively shaken when they found that the government intended to use the law as the basis of an official rural mobilization effort. Moreover, to force their compliance and participation in this unionization campaign, Goulart withheld the official federal subsidy from the landowners' confederation. The CRB consequently found itself in the anomalous position of promoting syndical reorganization to its member associations to maintain its financial solvency while simultaneously repudiating the regime responsible for the distasteful policy.[52]

The resulting rapid increase in the number of rural organizations did not, however, imply grass roots autonomy for the camponeses. It was soon apparent that political protection from landowner oppression was to be purchased only at the cost of political dependence on urban leftist leaders and submission to their manipulation.[53] The campaign for improved rural conditions through syndicalization became another springboard for politicans working their way up the political system. Everyone, including the government, wished to establish control over what seemed certain to become a major new constituency and source of populist political support. The stakes were much enhanced by the active support of many leftist politicians, including the president, for suffrage reform giving illiterates the right to vote. Such a move would have dramatically increased the size of the rural electorate. But it promised little political independence to the potential <u>camponês</u> voters.

Resisting submission to the demands of official clientelistic cooperation was obviously unrewarding. The <u>ligas</u>, perhaps the most independent of the rural groups, were harassed rather seriously even as early as the parliamentary period when they adopted an anti-administration position on the plebiscite. Julião publicly opposed a return to the presidential system in 1963 and urged <u>liga</u> members to abstain from voting.[53] Shortly thereafter, Julião was thrown out of the Brazilian Socialist Party and later denied membership in the PTB.[54] Having fallen out of favor with the official leftist forces in power, the <u>ligas</u> were not invited to enjoy the benefits of its patronage. On November 23, 1963 the new labor minister Amaury Silva, called a meeting of ULTAB, Popular Action, and the PTB. In compliance with the provisions of the Rural Worker Law they were instructed to form the national Confederation of Agricultural Workers, CONTAG. Pointedly excluding the <u>ligas</u>, the new organization "brought together 263 legally recognized rural syndicates, 480 rural syndicates in the process of receiving legal status, and twenty-nine Federations of Rural Syndicates from nineteen of the Brazilian states."[55]

But if the ligas camponesas experienced autonomy only briefly, other groups enjoyed none at all. ULTAB from the very first was manipulated by the communist party as a complement to its urban policy. When CONTAG formed, the official federal endorsement stifled most of the independent tendencies of the member syndicates. The fate that had befallen urban labor afflicted the new camponês unions as well. Indeed, in bringing the camponeses under official control, the populist urban leadership, especially that of the PTB and minor leftist parties, used urban labor unions as an ally.[56] In the Brazilian political context modernization of rural relations clearly implied a new form of clientelistic exploitation by the political leadership. In the early 1960s, a number of political actors openly competed for control of rural labor. Among them were landowners, the left populist government of João Goulart, two factions of the Catholic church, and several individual political leaders. It is doubtful that the camponeses themselves ever figured as serious contenders for the control of their own destiny.

Landowner Interest Organization and Class Solidarity

The landowner leadership, aware for some time that modernization would eventually affect the traditional agrarian sector, was concerned that the process of transition not undermine the political authority and economic preeminence of the fazendeiros in the countryside.[58] They favored an agrarian policy that would provide traditional planters and latifundists the time and means to adapt their properties to modern capitalist commercial exploitation. This concern motivated early participation of the CRB in discussions of agrarian policy initiated by Jânio Quadros in 1961.[59] The official landowner position advocated the replacement of old forms of agrarian production with a new capitalist agriculture confirming the inviolability of private property. For the fazendeiros "land reform" signified not a redistribution of property, but the initiation of the poor into the ways of private enterprise. In their view, this was best accomplished not by special government distribution programs for landless camponeses or minifundia owners, but by camponês recourse to commercial loans for the purchase of land.[60] CRB president Iris Meinberg condemned expropriation as a waste of resources and an incentive to speculation and rural unrest.[61] He felt the capitalist transformation of agriculture should be undertaken with the aid of an extensive government program which would benefit the entire agrarian sector and not just the poor by providing agricultural credit, training and extension programs, tax incentives, price supports, agroindustrial development incentives, and colonization of virgin lands.[62] Finally, conceding that land was not always used efficiently by owners, the CRB guidelines admitted the possibility of taxing unproductive property.[63]

There were some indications, however, that this official CRB platform was presented by the leadership as a gruding attempt to accommodate to some inevitable change without alienating its traditional constituency. Edgar Teixeira Leite, spokesperson for the rural confederation for many years and probably its single most influential publicist, proposed to the National Economic Council in July 1961 that the term "agrarian reform" be stripped of its negative redistributive connotations and rendered more acceptable to conservative landowners.[64] However, his suggestion that agrarian reform be redefined as "everything that aims at benefitting agriculture" seemed less an argument for land reform than an admission that many landowners were not ready for the CRB's progressive, capitalist proposals. In fact, while planters already involved in commercial export farming found these plans unexceptional, traditional latifundists thought them threatening to the old patriarchal order.

With Goulart's succession to the presidency and the accentuation of the land reform controversy, the landowners confederation found itself in a particularly unhappy situation. Jango's land reform plans and rural mobilization drive placed the confederation in the uncomfortable position of depending financially and politically on an executive apparently bent on destroying the power and coherence of the landed sector. Charges by some planters, such as the wealthy coffee growers of the Brazilian Rural Society (SRB) that the official confederation leadership consisted of government errand boys appeared to have some merit.[65] The SRB complained that the official agrarian leadership, no less _peleguista_ or subservient than that of labor, subsisted on the contributions of large planters while servily supporting government policies inimical to grower interests.[66]

However, the confederation could do little to alter its legally established relationship to the government. In theory, the general membership of the confederation elected the leaders representing the agricultural sector to the government. In fact, a candidate's political acceptability to the government served as the single most important criterion for his selection as an official. The undisguised political dependence of the confederation on the government caused it to be perceived by landowners generally as an unreliable defender of planter interests against official policies. Consequently, the active membership of the rural confederation tended to be small, as indicated by table 2-3. At a time when the employable rural population approximated twenty-five million people, associational membership consisted of approximately one-tenth of one percent of the total.

Table 2-3

MEMBERSHIP, BRAZILIAN RURAL CONFEDERATION

Year	Number of Associations	Number of Members
1946	108	18,453
1950	213	32,284
1955	1,130	179,558
1960	1,802	240,129
1961	1,867	229,034
1966	2,087	317,866

Source: Agricultura Brasileira, p.6.

The rural confederation's unenviable position between a threatening government and a contemptuous constituency underscored the special problems the CRB's official status generated for the leadership when it attempted to influence the conduct of government policy. Only official confederations were legally recognized as representatives of their sector's interests. But the official interest structure served more as a conduit for government views to the organized sectors than it did for the expression of the membership's opinions and needs. In a system which heavily stressed executive prerogatives in patronage and decision making, a president hostile to planter interests, as was João Goulart, effectively closed off that sector's access to the single most important official source of policy making. Before the 1963 plebiscite on parliamentarism, when he clearly needed conservative support for advancing the date of the referendum, Jango had made an effort to ingratiate himself with the landowners. In his single formal meeting with representatives of the "patronal" class in 1962, he assured them of his respect for private property and moderation. Following the restoration of the presidential system, he appeared to have reconsidered his need for the planters' support. As Goulart's reliance on radical mass politics increased, so did the distance between him and the landowners. The president saw no further utility in meetings or exchanges.[68]

The planters, in fact, seemed able to do little to neutralize the land reform threat while working within a framework which automatically gave the executive an upper hand. Even in the face of a serious challenge to their security, landowner interests demonstrated limited capacity to organize effectively for influencing a specific policy under legislative consideration. They were rather ineffectual as an interest group, as is demonstrated by later discussion in this study of the Congress and the policy process. Their power to influence policy, however inimical to their interests, was undercut by the state regulated interest structure and the susceptibility of clientelistic politics to central manipulation and patronage. Yet, paradoxically, as a major pillar of the traditional political order, the planter class could muster considerable power in defense of that order. It was curiously like an army regiment armed with no small or intermediate weapons and carrying only major destructive artillery. Although increasingly ineffective when defending its particular interests in battle, it nevertheless played a decisive role in winning the war in which it shared a stake with other conservative elites. The planter class did, in fact, literally arm itself in the defense of the patrimonial state and found ready allies in the defense of the political order.[69]

The willingness of other groups to join the fazendeiros in the defense of private property was based on their perception of a common political threat and not on any special sympathy for landowners or their problems. Concern over the agricultural bottleneck in the developmental scheme may have been widespread among economists and planners, but it enjoyed little currency in Brazilian business circles. Business representatives generally admitted having little knowledge of agriculture and perceiving no particular relationship between the performance of their particular sector and agriculture. The consequently felt little motivation for becoming involved in the technicalities of agrarian discussions.[70]

When in rare instances individual business leaders did demonstrate an interest in rural problems, they generally showed little concern for the poverty and exploitative in which the rural masses lived. Antônio Delfim Neto, a paulista economist destined to become minister of finance under presidents Costa e Silva and Garrastazú Médici following the 1964 revolution, typified knowledgeable business opinion at the time. Observing that the agricultural crisis was blown entirely out of proportion, he pointed out that the agrarian growth rate was 4.2 percent in 1963 -- an entirely acceptable figure, in his view, considering that the population was expanding at a rate of 2.8 percent. He categorically opposed any land redistribution program and maintained that agrarian problems could be alleviated by means of education, health, and industrialization programs.[71]

Only in one instance did the agrarian problem receive thoughtful attention from business leaders. The newly formed IPES (Institute for Social Research and Study) brought together business and military leadership to review systematically Brazil's national developmental problems.[72] A handsome volume on land reform figured as one of its most outstanding achievements.[73] This volume's significance extended well beyond the fact that a military industrial brain trust had produced a major review of the agrarian problem and proposed solutions. Rather, it lay in the fact that soon thereafter IPES members became officials of the 1964 military government and the agrarian study became the basis of an agrarian reform law enacted by the military regime in 1964.

But in the early sixties, such specific interest in the complexity of agricultural economics and social relations was rare.[74] The intense concern of conservative elites over the possible consequences of land reform was motivated primarily by political considerations. Thomas Pompeu Accioli Borges, Brazilian representative of the United Nations Food and Agricultural Organization, observed that despite passing reference to the desirability of a land reform to expand the internal market, the employer's group staunchly opposed an agrarian reform law. Whatever its potential benefits, they perceived it as a means to limit individual control over private property.[75] Speaking for the Federation of Commercial Associations of Brazil, Afrânio de Carvalho condemned the Goulart proposal for undermining democracy and making "a tabula rasa of the constitutional principles of property and free enterprise." The government should consequently adopt a substitute policy "in which implementation of the reform would be more on the basis of individual initiative than of state action."[76] The organization's president, Paulo de Almeida Barbosa expressed his concern more bluntly, saying that the Goulart proposal for a redistribution of property would lead to communism.[77]

This opinion was fully shared by the conservative wing of the Catholic church, which dissociated itself from the views of reformists such as Dom Helder Câmara, the bishop of Recife, and other clerics advocating social and economic reform. In a well publicized book attacking land reform (Agrarian Reform, a Matter of Conscience), three bishops and two lay persons movingly, if inaccurately, depicted the landowner as a hardworking man who acquired his property by the sweat of his brow. Arguing from a classically corporatist position, they appealed for the preservation of traditional social and economic distinctions since national well being depended on the "intimate cooperation /resulting from/ prudent and harmonious /sectoral/ differentiation. It is on this that social peace is founded."[78] Lest their argument be perceived as no more than a moral appeal, in a subsequent publication they suggested that anyone participating in a land reform program could be excommunicated.[79]

Within the armed forces, as within the church, the range of opinion on land reform varied considerably. The military as an institution was not single-mindedly opposed to a reform program. Indeed, Jango found support for his reformist goals among prominent figures within the top brass, such as General Segadas Viana, Admiral Angelo Nolasco, Brigadier General Clovis Travassos, General Machado Lopes, and General Pery Bevilacqua. In a more conservative, developmentalist vein, some military officials played an important role in IPES and contributing to its studies. But the weight of military opinion did not seem to be on the president's side. A study of the land reform issued by the alumni of the National War College favored an evolutionary agrarian policy and condemned drastic redistributive measures.[80] This attitude seemed closely related to the evidence of rising social unrest.[81] Overall, military concern with land reform mirrored a primary preoccupation with the ultimate political consequences of a policy which would challenge the established order, contribute to a lessening of political control over the masses and lead to a radical syndicalist regime.

This concern, shared equally by landowners and other employer groups, provided the basis for conspiratorial activity by the "producing classes" against the Goulart administration. Jango's program did not just threaten the standing of one sector of the economy in relationship to the others (as for instance, was the case earlier when agriculture bore the financial burden for industrialization). By attacking private property and encouraging lower class unrest, his land reform program imperilled the security and position of all the elites. Always uneasy about Goulart's succession to the presidency, conservative opposition began to plot the demise of his administration under the cover of the Superior Council of Producing Classes (CONCLAP), the peak employers' confederation. CONCLAP held monthly meetings in the year preceding Goulart's fall, and played an important role in cooperating with the church and other groups in mobilizing public opinion and organizing anti-government demonstrations.[82]

As Jango eventually abandoned any effort to deal with the conservative constraints on presidential authority, he began to take unilateral action to initiate reforms which the Congress had previously balked at passing. The armed forces watched the rising tide of social disorder and mass unrest with growing apprehension. Hard line opponents of Jango had long been plotting an overthrow among themselves. They now gained adherents from among the constitutionalists who had favored an orderly succession following Quadros' resignation in 1961. Concern over the crisis of the state was clearly superseding preoccupation with constitutionalism. Goulart sealed his own fate when he supported military unionization and interferred directly with the authority of commanding officers. This coalesced his military and civilian opposition and precipitated a coup against him.

Given the furor Goulart's proposal for land reform caused in conservative circles and the role it played in his overthrow, it may seem initially paradoxical that one of the first acts of the new military regime of General Humberto Castelo Branco was the passage of an agrarian reform law. Like Goulart's proposal, it aimed to transform the traditional rural economy. But Castelo's land law differed from that of his predecessor's radical redistributive proposal in its emphasis on modernization within an explicitly capitalist mode. Ultimately, the major issue raised by the agrarian controversy was not whether the traditional, socially exploitative and economically backward rural arrangements could be preserved. Rather, it was whether in making the transition to the modern era the landed class would preserve its status and prerogatives. The accomodationist process of development pursued by the corporatist capitalist state required the planters to share power with other, industrial and technological elites at the top of the socioeconomic pyramid. But it maintained the statist authority and elitist stratification system of the traditional political and social orders. The alternative solution represented by João Goulart was ultimately no less statist. But state power would be exercised by a militant vanguard in the name of, although not necessarily for, the masses, who would supplant the traditional elites as the new sociopolitical status group.

NOTES

1. See especially Anthony Leeds' insightful essay, "Brazilian Careers and Social Structure: An Evolutionary Model and Case Study," American Anthropologist, 66, Part I (1964), 1321-47.

2. Raymundo Faoro, Os Donos do Poder. A Formação do Patronato Político Brasileiro (Pôrto Alegre: Editôra Globo, 1958), pp. 44-45.

3. Faoro, p. 15, and Caio Prado Júnior, The Colonial Background of Modern Brazil (Berkeley: University of California Press, 1967), pp. 134-138.

4. Warren Dean, "The Problem of Latifundia in Nineteenth Century Brazil," Hispanic American Historical Review, (November 1971), p. 607.

5. Two particularly excellent discussions of this subject are Faoro and João Camilo de Oliveira Torres, A Democracia Coroada (Rio de Janeiro: Livraria José Olympio, 1957).

6. For an extensive treatment of this subject, see S.M. Eisenstadt, The Political Systems of Empires (New York: The Free Press, 1969). See also Barrington Moore, Jr., The Social Origins of Dictatorship and Democracy. Lord and Peasant in the Making of the Modern World (Boston: Beacon Press, 1966), chapter 4, "The Decay of Imperial China and the Origins of the Communist Variant."

7. Eisenstadt, pp. 14, 15, and 21.

8. João Camilo de Oliveira Torres, Estratificação Social no Brasil (São Paulo: Difusão Europeia do Livro, 1965), p.45. See also Juarez Rubens Brandão Lopez,, A Crise do Brasil Arcaico (São Paulo: Difusão Europeia do Livro, 1967).

9. For a discussion of coronelismo, Victor Nunes Leal's Coronelismo, Enxada e Voto (Rio de Janeiro: Livraria Forense, 1949) continues to be the best work on the subject, although more recent works are available. See, for instance, Marcos Vinicios Vilaça and Roberto Cavalcanti de Albuquerque, Coronel, Coroneis (Rio de Janeiro: Ediçoẽs Tempo Brasileiro, 1965). For a fine study of Rio Grande do Sul during the republican era see Joseph L. Love, Rio Grande do Sul and Brazilian Regionalism, 1882-1930 (Stanford, Cal.: Stanford University Press, 1971).

10. See Stanley Stein, Vassouras, A Brazilian Coffee County, 1850-1900 (Cambridge, Mass: Harvard University Press, 1957), and Gilberto Freyre, Ordem e Progresso (Rio de Janeiro: Editôra José Olympio, 1959). Alberto Passos Guimaraẽs, Quatro Séculos de Latifundio (Rio de Janeiro: Paz e Terra, 1968) deals specifically with these dependency relations in chapter 4.

11. For an in depth discussion of the Vargas regime, and especially of the beginning of the Estado Nôvo, see Robert M.

Levine, *The Vargas Regime: The Critical Years, 1934-1938* (New York: Columbia University Press, 1970). See also John W. F. Dulles, *Vargas of Brazil: A Political Biography* (Austin: The University of Texas Press, 1967).

12. Levine, pp. 14-15.

13. Helio Jaguaribe, *Economic and Political Development. A Theoretical Approach and a Brazilian Case Study* (Cambridge, Mass.: Harvard University Press, 1968), p. 144. See also his "A Crise Brasileira," *Cadernos de Nosso Tempo*, No. 1 (October-December 1953).

14. *Economic and Political Development*, p. 143.

15. Ibid., p. 144.

16. Philippe C. Schmitter's *Interest Conflict and Political Change in Brazil* (Berkeley: The University of California Press, 1971) provides the most comprehensive study of interest organization in Brazil.

17. The code, as Schmitter explains, "upheld voluntary membership, *sindicalismo único* (limiting recognition to one sindicato for each profession), representation of professional categories . . ., separate but equal treatment and parallel organization of workers and employers, and a series of government controls coordinating the activities of the associations and subordinating them to rational interests." It also introduced "a system of membership categories, a syndical tax, a comprehensive system of labor courts, and a minimum wage law." Ibid., p. 115.

18. John Wirth's *The Politics of Brazilian Development, 1930-1954* (Stanford, Cal.: The Stanford University Press, 1970) provides an overview of Vargas' social and economic policies. For a case study of the transition from agriculture to industry, see Warren Dean, *The Industrialization of São Paulo 1880-1945* (Austin: The University of Texas Press, 1969). Broader discussions of Brazilian economic and industrial development are provided by Werner Baer, *Industrialization and Economic Development in Brazil* (Homewood, Ill.: Irwin, 1965), and Celso Furtado, *The Economic Growth of Brazil* (Berkeley: The University of California Press, 1963).

19. Levine, p.13.

20. These were based on Decree Law 7038 of November 10, 1944, and made explicit in Decree Law 8127 of October 24, 1945, which stated that every *município* was to have a rural association in which all who "practiced rural activities by profession" were

qualified for membership.

21. Arno Schilling, "Sindicalização Rural" (Mimeo, Pôrto Alegre, 1969), p. 17.

22. A general discussion of Brazilian Politics from 1930 to 1964 can be found in Thomas E. Skidmore, Politics in Brazil, 1930-1964 (New York: Oxford University Press, 1967).

23. For a discussion of Brazilian political parties during this period see Phyllis Jane Peterson, "Brazilian Political Parties: Formation, Organization, and Leadership, 1945-1959" (unpublished Ph.D. dissertation, University of Michigan, 1962), and Marta Cehelsky, "The Brazilian Political Party System, 1945-1964. A Comparison With the Post-Independence Party System of India" (typescript, 1967).

24. Literally, a pelego is a sheepskin placed under a saddle. But, as the Pequeno Dicionario Brasileiro da Lingua Portuguesa explains, colloquially, it is a term used for "the Ministry of Labor's more or less covert agents in labor unions." Tenth edition, compiled by Aurelio Buarque de Hollanda Ferreira with José Baptista da Luz (Rio de Janeiro: Editôra Civilização Brasileira, 1963), p. 912.

25. Paulo Singer, "A Politica das Classes Dominantes," in Octavio Ianni, et al., Política e Revolução Social no Brasil (Rio de Janeiro: Civilização Brasileira, 1964), p. 74. See also Francisco Weffort, Politica de Massas," in the same volume and his "Raizes Sociais do Populismo em São Paulo," Revista Civilização Brasileira I (No. 2, 1965), and Juarez R.B. Lopez, Desenvolvimento e Mudança Social (São Paulo: Companhia Editôra Nacional, 1968), and Leeds, "Brazilian Careers and Social Structure."

26. Glaucio Ary Dillon Soares in "The Sociology of Uneven Development," in Irving Louis Horowitz, editor, Revolution in Brazil (New York: Dutton), 1964 argues that urbanization and industrialization, which are associated with the weakening of traditional ties, correlate positively with the rise of disciplined "ideological parties" and a relatively lower ratio of opportunistic party alliances. Juarez Lopez suggests ("Desenvolvimento," p. 229, n.4) somewhat more realistically that it is more probable that the type of political organization and style referred to by Soares is not the result of new economic and ideological interests, but merely an instrumental response on the part of politicians attempting to attract a new type of electoral support.

27. The one major work on populism in English is Ghita Ionescu and Ernest Gellner, editors, Populism, its Meanings

and National Characteristics (London: Weidenfeld and Nicolson, 1969). The chapter on Latin America by Alistair Hennessy does little, however, to enhance our understanding of Brazilian populism. More useful is Torcuato di Tella's "Populism in Latin America" in Claudio Veliz, editor, Obstacles to Change in Latin America (New York: Oxford University Press, 1965).

28. See particularly Jaguaribe's analysis of these developments in Economic and Political Development, especially chapter 10, "The Process of Development," and chapter 12, "The New Structural Crisis."

29. Quadros received 5,636,623 votes, or 48.29 percent of the 11,679,679 valid votes cast. Institute for the Comparative Study of Political Systems, Brazil Election Factbook Number 2. September 1965 (Washington, D.C.: ICOPS, 1965), p. 56.

30. Instituto Brasileiro de Reforma Agraria (IBRA), Estrutura Agrária Brasileira (Rio de Janeiro: IBRA, 1967).

31. The body of literature on agricultural conditions in Brazil, and especially the Northeast, is enormous. The Bibliografia sobre Reforma Agrária published by the Instituto de Ciencias Sociais (Rio de Janeiro: Universidade do Brasil, 1962) listed 1,164 publications on the subject. Among the best sources are: Passos Guimarães, Quatro Séculos de Latifundio, Manuel Correia de Andrade, A Terra e o Homem no Nordeste (São Paulo: Editôra Brasiliense, 1963), Euclides da Cunha, Rebellion in the Backlands (Chicago: University of Chicago Press, 1944), Antônio Callado, Os Industriais da Seca e os "Galileus de Pernambuco," (Rio de Janeiro: Civilização Brasileira, 1960), and Manuel Diegues Júnior, População e Açucar no Nordeste do Brasil (Rio de Janeiro: Comissão Nacional de Alimentação, 1965).

32. Instituto Brasileiro de Geografia e Estatistica, Anuario Estatístico do Brasil (Rio de Janeiro: 1954-1976).

33. CIDA, Land Tenure Conditions and Socio-Economic Development in Brazil (Washington, D.C.: Pan American Union, 1963), p. 24.

34. Armin K. Ludwig and Harry W. Taylor, Brazil's New Agrarian Reform. An Evaluation of its Property Classification and Tax Systems (New York: Praeger, 1969), p.3. See also essays by Julian Chacel and Gordon Smith in Howard Ellis, ed., The Economy of Brazil (Berkley: The University of California Press, 1970), and Henrique de Barros, A Estrutura Agrária como Obstáculo a Ação Agronômica. A Reforma Agrária como Problema Econômico (São Paulo: Escola de Sociologia e Política de São Paulo, 1954). Warren Dean notes this type of concern as early

as the 1920s and 1930s. Industrialization of São Paulo, pp. 130-133.

35. Between 1960 and 1963 alone, eight nations complied by passing agrarian reform laws. They were: Chile, Colombia, Costa Rica, Dominican Republic, Guatemala, Nicaragua, Panama, and Venezuela.

36. As Samuel Huntington has observed, "The ability of the political system to survive and of its government to remain stable depends upon its capacity to counter /the/ revolutionary appeal /of urban groups/ and to bring the peasants into politics on the side of the system." Political Order in Changing Societies (New Haven: Yale University Press, 1968), p. 292.

37. The best discussion of labor in Brazil is to be found in Kenneth P. Erickson, The Brazilian Corporative State and Working Class Politics (Berkeley: University of California Press, 1977).

38. See Arno Schilling, passim, Schmitter, chapter 8, and Edgar Teixeira Leite, "Aspectos da Sindicalização Rural no Brasil," Jurídica No. 31 (abril-junho 1966).

39. Clodomir Moraes, "Peasant Leagues in Brazil," In Rodolfo Stavenhagen, editor, Agrarian Problems and Peasant Movements in Latin America (New York: Doubleday, 1970), pp. 462-464. See also Cynthia N. Hewitt, "Brazil: The Peasant Movement of Pernambuco, 1961-1964," in Henry A. Landsberger, editor, Latin American Peasant Movements (Ithaca, N.Y.: Cornell University Press, 1969), pp.324-398, and Mary E. Wilkie, "A Report on the Rural Syndicates of Pernambuco" (Mimeo, Rio de Janeiro, Centro de Pesquisas em Ciências Sociais, 1964).

40. Ibid., p. 465.

41. Ibid., pp. 477-78. Ironically, the sympathy of the state government had negative consequences for the ligas according to Moraes. "Once given title to their land by the state, the Galileia peasants lost interest in the politics of the agrarian struggle." The Galiléia liga, which until this time had been the center of the organizational effort, dwindled to a few dozen quarelling members by 1961.

42. Ibid., p. 491.

43. Ibid., p. 482.

44. Wilkie, p. 7.

45. Gleba, Vol. 8, No. 85 (1962), p. 37.

46. Moraes., pp. 497-498.

47. Originally a PTB deputy from the state of Rio de Janeiro, Ferrari ran as one of Jânio Quadros' two vice presidential candidates, and lost. Disillusioned with the politics within the PTB and by the PTB's conduct in the national political arena, he formed his own party, the Labor Renovation Movement (MTR). His death in an airplane crash in 1963 cut short a promising political career.

48. Estatuto do Trabalhador Rural, Title I, Art. 1, and 2. Adriano Campanhole, editor, Legislação Agrária (São Paulo: Editôra Atlas, 1969.)

49. Adolpho Puggina, Reforma Agrária. A Reforma das Reformas (Pôrto Alegre: FETAG, 1968) p. 16.

50. Confederação Rural Brasileira, "Relatôrio das Atividades da Confederação Rural Brasileira em 1965" (mimeo, Rio de Janeiro, 1965), pp. 1, 2. See also, Teixeira Leite, "Aspectos da Sindicalização," p.4, and his "Aspectos do Complexo Agrário Brasileiro," Carta Mensal (Orgão do Conselho Técnico da Confederação Nacional da Industria, Vol. 15, No. 180 (1970), p. 13.

51. Goulart's support for the bill initially was quite lukewarm. It was not until after its passage that he appeared to realize fully its political potential. Correio da Manhã, March 6, 1963, p. 6. Cited hereafter as CM.

52. For a discussion of the CRB and the syndicalization issue see Teixeira Leite, "Aspectos da Sindicalização," and Confederacao Rural Brasileira, "Sindicalização Rural," (mimeo, Rio de Janeiro, n.d.).

53. The political potential of the campanonês organization has been the subject of considerable controversy. Anthony Leeds argues that the relationship between Julião and the ligas was basically clientelistic and paternalistic and that Julião was a typical elitist Brazilian politician in a new ideological disguise. "Brazil and the Myth of Francisco Julião," in Joseph Maier and Richard W. Weatherhead, editors, The Politics of Change in Latin America (New York: Praeger, 1964). Benno Galjert takes a similar position in a debate with Gerrit Huizer in América Latina. Huizer, in contrast, sees the organizational activity among the camponeses as the beginning of class consciousness and independent political action. Benno Galjert, "Class and 'Following' in Rural Brazil, "América Latina, Vol. 7, No. 3 (julho-septembro 1964); Gerrit Huizer, "Some Notes on Community Development and Social Research," América Latina, Vol. 8, No. 3 (julho-septembro 1965).

54. Francisco Julião, editor, Ligas Camponesas: Outubro 1962 -- Abril 1964 (Cuernavaca: CIDOC, 1969). The following message was typical of his campaign: "Under the presidential regime, 70% of the land was in the hands of 2% of the latifundists. Under the parliamentary regime, nothing has changed. Therefore, there is no difference /between the two/. There is another option. A vote for agrarian reform is not to vote in the plebiscite." Ligas, p. 63.

55. Jornal do Brasil, January 3, 1963, p. 1, and January 6, 1963, p. 3. Cited hereafter as J B

56. See, for example, the Correio da Manha, June 4, 1963, p. 16, for a review of the General Confederation of Labor's plans for strikes and bus caravans, and July 11, 1963, p. 4 for an account of the CGT's organization of the week of Basic Reforms.

57. Moraes, p. 492.

58. Teixeira Leite, "Aspectos do Complexo Agrário," p. 7.

59. Officially, the CRB deplored what it referred to as the chronic official neglect of agriculture. (See in particular, CRB, "A Agricultura Brasileira, Diretrizes para um Plano de Ação." Memorial da CRB as Exmo. Senhor Presidente da Republica, Doutor Jânio da Silva Quadros. Gleba, Marco 1961, p. 8; and Ben Hur Raposo, A Reforma Agrária para o Brasil (Rio de Janeiro: Fondo de Cultura, 1965), pp. 24, 25). In so doing, it conveniently ignored the possibility that latifundio owners might have found this neglect particularly advantageous in the short term.

60. Teixeira Leite, "Reforma Agrária Brasileira. Destinação Econômica e Social da Terra," Observações sobre o Ante-Projeto da Comissão Especial (mimeo, Rio de Janeiro, Conselho Nacional de Economia, n.d.), p. 16.

61. CRB, "A Agricultura Brasileira," pp. 25, 26.

62. Ibid., pp. 11, 39, 40, and passim. See also Gleba, Vol. 7, nos. 74-77 (1961), p. 11, and J B , July 28, 1961, p. 8.

63. "A Agricultura Brasileira," pp.25-26.

64. "Reforma Agrária, Destinação, p.4.

65. In interviews I conducted in São Paulo, SRB representatives did little to hide their contempt for the official leadership.

66. The notion that the leadership of the official employers' group is subservient to and manipulated by the state has gained greater currency with the study of Brazilian corporatism. Faoro was an early advocate of this view. More recently, Schmitter and Erickson have taken this position.

67. During interviews I conducted, confederation leaders stressed that it was pointless to elect someone of whom the government did not approve. Schmitter makes a similar observation, indicating that official supervision discourages grass roots participation.

68. C M , June 22, 1963, p. 15.

69. J.B., July 29, 1961, p. 3. The rumor reported by the Jornal do Brasil was substantiated in interviews I conducted with landowners, particularly in Rio Grande do Sul and Minas Gerais.

70. The reaction of a high official of the National Confederation of Industries to my request for an interview on agrarian policy was somewhat more extreme than most but not atypical. He felt sure at first that while looking for the National Confederation of Agriculture, as the CRB was retitled in 1966, I had erroneously wandered into the wrong confederation offices.

71. Antônio Delfim Neto, "Agricultura e Desenvolvimento," Mundo Econômico, No. 10 (1967), p. 5. See also the Estado de São Paulo, October 20, 1963 for a declaration of the Technical Council of Social and Political Economy, signed by Delfim and other prominent economists, industrialists, and businessmen.

72. Two branches of IPES were established in 1962, one in São Paulo, the other in Rio de Janeiro. The carioca branch functioned as a research group and survived the 1964 crisis. The paulista group, which functioned more as a political pressure group and organizing center for anti-Goulart demonstrations and other activities ceased to function after the 1964 military take-over. A review of IPES membership lists and executive committee meeting minutes read like a "who's who" in Brazilian government. IPES files, typescript and manuscript, 1962-1966, passim.

73. Instituto de Pesquisas e Estudos Sociais, A Reforma Agrária: Problemas, Bases, e Soluções (Rio de Janeiro: IPES, 1964).

74. Robert Kaufman, Chile's Agrarian Reform (Washington, D.C.: ICOPS, 19 p. 36).

75. Thomas Pompeu de Accioli Borges, "Novos Rumos para a Reforma Agrária Brasileira" (typescript, Rio de Janeiro, 1968, internal document of the Grupo de Trabalho Sobre Reforma Agrária), p.6.

76. C M , May 5,1963, Caderno 2, p. 20.

77. Paulo de Almeida Barbosa, quoted in A Gazeta (São Paulo), May 8, 1963. Also, see A Folha de São Paulo, May 16, 1963 for similar statements by the Federation of Industries of São Paulo.

78. Dom Orlando Rodriguez, Dom Antônio de Castro Maier, Dom Geraldo Proença Sigaud, Plínio Correa de Oliveira and Luiz Mendonça Freitas, Reforma Agrária, Questão de Consciencia (São Paulo: Editôra Vera Cruz, 1960), p. 20.

79. Dom Orlando Rodriguez, et al., Declaração do Morro Alto. Programa de Política Agrária Conforme os Princípios de Reforma Agrária, Questão de Consciencia (São Paulo: Editôra Vera Cruz, 1964), p. 10.

80. Accioli, "Novos Rumos," p. 5.

81. J B , February 4, 1962, p. 3. Also see Visão, May 31, 1963, p. 11 for a statement on the subject by General Kruel.

82. Schmitter, p. 197. Also see pp. 195 for the origins of CONCLAP.

3. Presidential Politics and Land Reform

Although they differed sharply in style, personality, and the general tenor of their administration, João Goulart and Humberto Castelo Branco coincided in their perception of land reform as one of the principal issues of the time. In confronting land reform, they grappled with a political and economic problem that could no longer be postponed. Their respective programs, while implying distinct consequences for the political system, both recognized that the old Brazilian agricultural order was doomed.

Despite their apparent ideological differences, Goulart and Castelo also concurred on a number of the major measures they considered necessary for the resolution of the land reform problem. Specifically, both insisted that the land statute be accompanied by a constitutional amendment which would make it possible to pay for expropriated land in bonds. Both considered expropriation a necessary feature of any land reform program. Neither reduced the agrarian problem to simple economic terms, but emphasized instead its profound social dimension. Finally, both presidents favored an agrarian policy consisting of a combination of land redistribution, colonization, and agricultural support measures. The two presidents diverged principally in their perceptions of the true purpose of land reform. For Castelo it was the modernization of agriculture in a capitalist framework; for Jango, it was the restructuring of the social order.

AGRARIAN PROPOSALS

Despite the furor it caused, Goulart's land reform proposal was not exceptionally innovative. Nearly two hundred agrarian bills were introduced in the Congress in the course of Brazilian history. In the sixties alone, the reports, conference resolutions, vague commitments, and proposals were transformed into twelve major bills and laws, some radical, other revisionist.[1] These twelve major proposals are listed in table 3-1, indicating sponsorship of the measure, its purpose, and the action taken on it. Except for their divergence on the issues of the means and justification for the expropriation of property, the proposals are similar in many respects. The definition of priorities and objectives usually included a statement about social justice and the need to create a class of independent middle class farmers. Frequently, there would follow a list of measures aimed at stimulating agricultural production. Among these, progressive taxation was a favored strategy. By contrast, Brizola's and Goulart's idea of forced leasing found support only among the radical left politicians. All the proposals suggested some form of land expropriation and redistribution and extensive programs of colonization, agricultural extension, credit, and technical assistance.

The basic similarity of the bills and proposals is not surprising. First of all, they reflected the temper, orientation, and knowledge of the times and of their sponsors. In the second place, they were cumulative. Earlier bills served as a basis for the elaboration of new ones. Finally, all bills written after 1961 were strongly influenced by the work of the Milton Campos commission. Named informally for its coordinator, Senator Milton Campos, the Special Commission for Agrarian Reform was established by President Quadros in May 1961.[2] Its purpose was to study the agricultural situation in Brazil and to build on the work begun by the National Commission for Agricultural Policy established by Getúlio Vargas in 1951. The Campos commission was charged with recommending legislative and executive measures necessary to alter the land tenure system, promote rural justice, and increase agricultural productivity.[3] The commission's findings, advocating a combination of land reform and agricultural assistance, influenced all subsequent legislation. Specifically, all ensuing proposals supported the following measures: 1) the creation of a productive farming class out of the impoverished and often landless camponeses and rural workers; 2) the alteration of land use patterns to bring unused land under cultivation; 3) colonization of available unused land; and 4) the improvement of agricultural productivity through credit, technical assistance, and extension programs. The Campos commission also recommended the creation of a Superintendency for Agrarian Reform.

Despite these similarities, the areas of disagreement among the agrarian proposals of the 1960s were not minor either in terms of their importance or in the degree of controversy they generated. Controversy focused on a constitutional amendment permit-

Table 3-1

MAJOR AGRARIAN LEGISLATION, 1960-1970

Sponsor	Proposal	Purpose	Action Taken
Dep. Fernando Ferrari, PTB/MTR Rio de Janeiro May, 1961	Rural Worker Law	Protection of rights of rural workers, right to unionize, regulation of contracts, work conditions, social security	Enacted into law as law No.4214, March 2, 1963
Dep. José Joffily, PSD, Paraíba, July, 1961	Agrarian Reform Bill	Moderate redistribution within confines of constitution; extension, colonization programs	None
Dep. Gileno de Carli, PSD, São Paulo, July, 1961	Agrarian Reform Bill	Emphasis on colonization, productivity, credit	None
Sen. Milton Campos, UDN, Minas Gerais, August, 1962	Agrarian Reform Bill	Creation of farmer class; similar to Joffily proposal, better elaborated	Passed by Senate Dec. 1962, defeated by Chamber, Aug.1963

Dep. Leonel Brizola, PTB, Rio Grande do Sul, March, 1963	Agrarian Reform Bill	Radical alteration of tenure system based on expropriation with alteration of constitution	None
Pres. João Goulart, March, 1963	Agrarian Reform Bill	Radical land redistribution based on constitutional amendment	Action depended on amendment, below
Pres. João Goulart, April, 1963	Constitutional Amendment	Make possible expropriation of land payable in bonds, maximum indexation ten per cent	Rejected October, 1963
Dep. Aniz Badra, PDC, São Paulo, August, 1963	Agrarian Reform Bill	Create middle-class farmers; closely resembled Campos bill	Passed only by Chamber, April, 1964
Pres. João Goulart, March 13, 1964	Expropriation Decree	Expropriate property bordering roads, railroads, dams, within ten kilometers	Signed by President March 13, 1964, based on Decree Law 3365, June 21, 1941
Pres. Castelo Branco, May, 1964	Constitutional Amendment	Make possible expropriation of land payable by fully indexed bonds	Passed as Amendment No. 10 to Constitution Nov. 6, 1964

Table 3-1 - Continued

Sponsor	Proposal	Purpose	Action Taken
Pres. Castelo Branco, May, 1964	Land Statute Proposal	Increase productivity, promote social justice in countryside, distribute land, colonization; heavy reliance on progressive taxation	Passed as Land Statute, Law No. 4504, Nov. 30, 1964
Pres. Costa e Silva, April, 1969	Institutional Act Number 9	Facilitate expropriation procedure, making it administrative, not court matter, regulate compliance with taxation	Signed by president, April, 1969
Pres. Emilio Garrastazú Médici, July, 1970, February, 1971	Decree Law No. 1110; Decree Law No. 68153	Abolish land reform and agrarian development institutes created in 1964. Substitute National Institute for Colonization and Agrarian Reform (INCRA) with an emphasis on colonization	Signed by president, July, 1970, February, 1971
Pres. Emilio Garrastazú Médici, July, 1971	Decree Law No. 1179	Create Program of Redistribution of Land and Stimulus to the Agro-Industry of the Northeast (PROTERRA); alters tax incentives system tied to land program. Focus: creation of agro-industry	Signed by president, July, 1971

Sources: Based on record of congressional debates, newspaper accounts, J. Motta Maia, _Iniciação a Reforma Agrária_ (Rio de Janeiro: Mabri, 1969), and Adriano Campanhôle and Hilton Lôbo Campanhôle, _Legislacao Agrária_ (São Paulo: Atlas, S.A., 1974, 6th edition).

ting land expropriation to be compensated in the form of long-term bonds rather than in cash. This would materially alter the relevant provisions of the extant 1946 constitution which made land expropriation both difficult and unfeasible because of its cost. Article 141, paragraph 16 stated:

> The right of property is guaranteed, except in cases of expropriation for reasons of public need, or utility, or for social benefit, by means of previous and just compensation in money. In the case of imminent danger, such as war, or internal disorder, the competent authorities may use private property, if the public good so requires, with the right to subsequent indeminization remaining assured.[4]

Although article 147 of the constitution provided that the use of property was subject to public welfare and that the state had the power to redistribute property, such expropriation was possible only on the basis of full payment in cash prior to the act of expropriation itself.

Under these rules, the funds required for a widespread expropriation program would have to be enormous and an agrarian reform bound by these restrictions would have a very limited application. By specifying the type and time of payment, the 1946 constitution precluded the use of long-term bonds, which would neither be negotiable as currency nor redeemable until a specified number of years had passed. Understandably, anyone advocating a comprehensive land reform within the existing framework would insist on a revision of the constitution. A constitutional amendment aimed at modifying the provisions on expropriation to permit a more rational, long range repayment program constituted the core issue of the debate on land reform and the bone of contention between the president and Congress.

The Legislative Process

To facilitate comprehension of the two presidents' relationships to Congress while trying to secure both a land reform law and an amendment to the constitution, it will be helpful to review briefly the constitutional framework of the Brazilian legislative process during the post World War II period.

According to the Brazilian constitution of 1946, bills could be introduced by the president and by any member or commission of either of the two houses of Congress, the Chamber of Deputies and the Senate. Within each house, twelve permanent committees exist to rule on specific matters, such as constitutional problems, finance, education, etc. The respective membership of these committees, which report on specific aspects of legislation under consideration, ranges from a handful in either house, to close to a hundred in the budget and commerce committee of the Chamber.[5] Until 1964, there was little difference in the type of bill that could be introduced by either house. Since the revolution, however, monetary bills can be introduced only by the president or the Chamber of Deputies. A bill proposed by the executive, both before and after the revolution, has had to be considered first by the Chamber, and if approved, passed on to the Senate. To become law, an ordinary bill must be passed by a majority vote in both houses, and signed by the president. A two-thirds vote of both houses is necessary to overrule a presidential veto.

The first decrees issued by the revolutionary government in 1964 altered the legislative process.

Article four of the first Institutional Act provided the following:

> The President of the Republic may send the National Congress bills on any subject, which must be acted on within thirty days . . . from day of receipt in the Chamber of Deputies and in equal time in the Federal Senate: . . . [if no action is taken] they will be considered [automatically] approved.

Furthermore:

> If he considers the matter urgent, the President of the Republic can call on the National Congress to consider the bill in a joint session in thirty days. . . .

If Congress failed to act within the time limit, the bill automatically became law.

Equally important, if not more so, were the changes introduced in the procedure for amending the constitution. Before April 1964, proposals for amendments could be introduced only by a fourth or more of the Chamber or of the Senate, or by over half of all state assemblies acting within two years' time.[6] After the revolution, the president himself could propose amendments. When the executive acted on this possibility and sent a proposed constitutional amendment to Congress, the national legislature was required to act on it within thirty days of its receipt. The amendment was approved if the proposal received an absolute majority of votes in both houses of Congress in two sessions held not more than ten days apart.

These differences in rules had a decisive impact on the manner in which Congress considered presidential bills before and after 1964. While Goulart was forced to resort to various means of applying political pressure to hasten the legislative process,

Castelo had considerably greater institutional leverage. Most of the latter's bills, although they could be amended and altered by Congress, automatically became law unless specifically rejected within thirty days. In the area of constitutional amendments, Castelo also had an advantage in that he himself could propose one, without the concomitant need to rely on his political party to secure the signatures of a fourth of the members of both houses. The thirty day time limit was also a clear incentive for Congress to take action of some kind. With these changes, the position of the executive in relation to Congress was strengthened. This did not mean, however, that the president could afford to ignore the legislature. Congress could defeat bills as well as approve them, and had not yet been reduced to a rubber stamp, as it would be in 1968.

JOÃO GOULART AND LAND REFORM

Jango's handling of the agrarian reform controversy was intimately related to his political standing. He fortuitously became president following Jânio's unexpected resignation and in the face of considerable political opposition. It was based on fears that Vargas' protege, who admired both Lenin and Argentine ex-president, Juan Perón, would favor the creation of a radical syndicalist regime. Goulart succeeded to office principally because the military was divided on whether to allow him to take power, and because there were strong currents of both military and civilian opinion supporting the preservation of constitutional legality. However, although the opposition could not prevent Goulart from taking power, it exacted a paralyzing compromise. Goulart took office, not as head of the presidential system established since 1946, but as the president of a new parliamentary regime designed to circumscribe the power of the chief executive.

While it lasted, the parliamentary framework indeed constrained the new president in the exercise of his powers. Jango's eventual success in having it abolished did not, however, prove an automatic means to effective executive authority. The more serious obstacles were not to be disposed of so easily. Most important among these difficulties was an institutional crisis rooted in the contradiction between the oligarchic distribution of political power and the populist requirements of the electoral system since 1946. The conditions of effective rule remained elitist and oriented toward informal negotiation among the economically and socially powerful members of the corporate elite. The presidential road to power, on the other hand, was based on populist mass appeal to an expanding electorate. As a consequence, the Brazilian president was elected to office by one constituency, which enabled him to "reign;" but he could "rule" effectively only with the support of another. To the extent that the policy process had to be conducted within this schizophrenic framework, discussion of fundamental issues dealing with the nature of the system tended to an impasse. The populist promises on one hand, and the corporatist elitism on the other, implied two mutually exclusive alternatives in the social definition of problem solving. Jânio Quadros' earlier attempts to eliminate this contradiction and to provide a common base for both election of officials and for their governing, ended in frustration and his resignation after seven months in office.

A second difficulty centered on the personality and political beliefs of João Goulart. Within a difficult institutional situation, Jango was regarded with utmost suspicion and distrust by established political forces, both in the anti-Vargas National Democratic Union (UDN) party and even in the Vargas-founded Social Democratic Party (PSD). Goulart's single important power base was in the labor unions and in the Brazilian Labor Party (PTB). In the eyes of the Brazilian political establishment, Jango's political career, labor affiliations, and apparently keen interest in the ideology and strategies of former Argentine president, Juan Perón, rendered him untrustworthy. Furthermore, he was perceived as a political opportunist who could not even be trusted to maintain any idological position with integrity. For conservatives and moderates alike, the only thing worse than a dogmatic ideological leftist, was an unprincipled, unpredictable, and opportunistic leftist. Since effective executive rule was premised on at least a tacit acceptance by these political and military elites, their disapproval meant that he was most unlikely to succeed where Jânio had recently failed.

A third difficulty, as Ronald Schneider points out, consisted in Goulart's having been "manufactured by Vargas as an instant national figure," and in lacking the experience normally gained by national politicians who had been governors and/or national legislators. "His hop-skip-and-jump career -- straight from the ranch to the cabinet, then on to the vice presidency, and accidental accession to power -- was all too apparent in his relations with the military."[7]

-- And, we might add, with most groups and institutions outside of labor.

Finally, these structural and situational difficulties were compounded by Goulart's self image and his perceptions of his own role as president. Goulart did not want to be known historically as the man who was constantly defeated by political circumstances. He wished to make an historical impact and to be remembered for some major contribution:[8]

> Often viewed as a weak personality for a major political leader, he was not prone to run risks for abstruse principles or causes in which he had no great stake. A shrewd political manipulator with no great vision and prone to look for the path of least resistance, Goulart was not, however, lacking ambitions that transcended the mere holding of office. . . . He did not wish to go down in history as a weak and indecisive man, unable to deal effectively with the problems of Brazil. He was not disposed either to become a powerless tool of the established commercial, industrial, and agricultural groups or to be upstaged. . . by a more authentic and popular figure on the left. . . . His irresoluteness stemmed from a lack of training in dealing with technical problems and a lack of patience in studying complex matters.[9]

As Schneider's assessment of the president's personality indicates, Goulart would have had trouble mastering the art of governing even in the best of circumstances. Yet he came to power under the worst possible conditions. As reflected in his handling of the agrarian reform bill, in his struggle with Congress, and his relationship with other groups he would not be able to rise above historical constraints or his personal limitations.

Goulart's brief presidential career can be divided into four distinct periods. The first period, that of the parliamentary regime, began with his inauguration on September 7, 1961 and ended with the return of the presidential system following the plebiscite of January 6, 1963. The second period, notable for his collaboration with the "positive left," lasted from January to June 1963. Then, from his June cabinet reshuffle to December of the same year constituted the third period, an interval with emphasis on radicalization, but without overstepping the limits of the opposition's political tolerance. The final period, from December 1963 to his ouster in March, was characterized by the abandonment of the established political process and a unilateral attempt to exploit radical mobilization strategies.

Parliamentary Interlude: September 1961 - January 1963

The fourteen months of the parliamentary regime were the calm before the storm. Although it had looked like the only solution possible at the time, parliamentarism was not, as it turned out, a very happy one. It may not have been directly responsible for increasing inflation, declining investment, flight of capital, slow down in economic activity, and increased social unrest. But the new system appeared to be incapable of confronting these problems. Goulart's claim that he could not possibly influence the situation or improve it while his hands were tied seemed plausible enough.

The parliamentary arrangement aggravated Goulart's difficulties with Congress. The president's own Brazilian Labor Party, the PTB, was a minority party, contending with an obviously hostile National Democratic Union, and a suspicious Social Democratic Party. The PSD might have been convinced to cooperate, but only in exchange for some direct benefit to itself. The conservative opposition, which included many pessedistas (PSD members), formed the Democratic Parliamentary Action coalition (ADP), to shore up the parliamentary regime as a means of circumscribing Goulart's influence. The president faced a challenge from the left as well in the form of an alliance between the followers of Deputy Fernando Ferrari of the state of Rio de Janeiro, and the compactos, or left wing of the PTB, which denounced Goulart's brand of politics for its lack of ideological consistency.[10] Ferrari, in fact, seemed to be challenging Goulart's leadership of the left and pushing for the formation of a new party, which would be a fusion of Ferrari's Labor Renovation Movement, the National Labor Party, and factions of the Christian Democratic and Brazilian Labor Parties.[11] Perhaps on a more embarrassing personal level to Goulart was the challenge to his leadership by his own brother-in-law, Leonel Brizola, governor of Rio Grande do Sul at the time. To make matters worse, it could not even be said with any degree of assurance that Goulart was actually in control of the National Liberation Front (FLN), organized as a leftist answer to the ADP. The efficacy of the FLN as a policy instrument was in any case questionable. While in theory representing a reformist position on behalf of the people, the FLN's effectiveness was impugned by its seeming irrelevance to the needs of the increasingly radicalized masses and its inability to deliver promised reforms.[12]

Two immediate political tasks dominated the agenda in the second half of 1962. One was the congressional interim election in October 1962. The second was the preparation of the plebiscite. Goulart concentrated on the plebiscite, paying relatively little attention to the bitterly contested election in which structural reforms were the main issue. The plebiscite had been originally scheduled for 1965 and Goulart intended to move it up by a full two years. His strategy was two-pronged. First, he deliberately undertook to allay the fears and suspicions of traditional and conservative sectors of opinion. While making pointed reference to growing social unrest and strikes, Goulart's piously conservative speeches emphasized the need for carefully prepared and rational reforms and for austerity measures to deal with the financial crisis. Second, he relied on the negative impression parliamentarism itself was creating. For Goulart the series of governmental crises and cabinet reforms served the purpose of demonstrating that the parliamentary system was unweidly, inefficient, and incapable of solving the pressing problems of the day. If not attended to, Goulart stressed, the impasse might result in revolution. Enough politicians and military figures were swayed by this argument and by the political and social unrest to have the plebiscite moved up to January 6, 1963.

Besides pressing for a return of the presidential system, which was perhaps, as Schneider says, Goulart's [illegible]le greatest accomplishment, the president was preparing another major project -- a program of "Basic Reforms." Far more interesting than the boring details of the financial crisis, "the idea of such reforms," Skidmore points out, "appeared to offer Jango the opportunity of making an historical reputation for himself and also a way of building his own political following."[13] The keystone of this program, which he launched on May Day in 1962, was land reform.

In emphasizing land reform, Goulart was taking advantage of an issue that had already achieved considerable public prominence. Internationally, continued aid from the Alliance for Progress was linked to enactment of a land reform law. This foreign pressure underscored a series of domestic events. The work of the Milton Campos commission urgently calling for an agrarian policy coincided with predictions of a poor harvest in 1962. Food shortages were already being experienced. Concern with the state of social unrest and the drop in agricultural productivity motivated several states to confront the issue on their own. Governor Carvalho Pinto of São Paulo, who at a later point would become Goulart's minister of finance, succeeded in having the _paulista_ legislature pass an Agricultural Revision Law in November 1961. The mildly reformist statute emphasized rural credit, technical assistance, and some colonization. A more radical redistributive bill would have stood little chance of passage in the face of opposition from the state's powerful commercial export sector.

Modest as it was, however, the new _paulista_ law generated some excitement and alarm. Not a few _paulistas_ perceived it as a dangerous encroachment on constitutional rights. Defenders of the rural status quo in other parts of the country viewed it as the first crack in the dyke of their social, economic, and political hegemony. Indeed, in a general sense, their assessment had some merit since there seemed to be a move afoot in various states to enact some sort of agricultural policy.[14] Brizola's agrarian reform activities, which included rural unionization and some land expropriation by the Gaucho Institute of Land Reform were perceived as especially threatening.

Since the major resource available to state legislatures and governors for inducing reforms was the power of taxation, the rural opposition mobilized a campaign against this potentially dangerous prerogative.

The ruralists' strategy was astute. They would have been most unwise to launch an anti-land reform campaign in an era when being against reforms was equivalent to being against motherhood.[15] Instead, the opposition operated from behind a more popular facade -- that of "municipalism." In essence a movement for decentralization of authority and financial powers, particularly the powers of taxation affecting rural property, municipalism argued for the devolution of these powers to local governing units. The ruralists reactivated the old campaign, and formed an alliance with the municipalists, who alone had never been able to achieve their aim. Congressional passage of Constitutional Amendment No. 5 on November 21, 1961, transferring the power of rural property taxation from states to municípios made any discussion of agrarian reform through state initiative academic. After the 230 to 4 vote in favor of the Senate-sponsored amendment was tallied in the Chamber of Deputies, one federal deputy, in a moment of candor, gloated over the "end of agrarian reform."[16] Clearly, if there were to be any land reform at all, it would have to come from the federal government.

As if in recognition of this fact, and also in preparation for what promised to be a stiff political battle, the annual governors' conference meeting in Araxá in early June of 1962 placed the discussion of agrarian reform high on its agenda. In spite of considerable opposition to a pronouncement of any kind, the conference in an official statement endorsed agrarian reform based, however, on the provisions of the constitution.[17] The radical and reformist governors, who opposed the official position taken by the conference, contended that any agrarian reform not based on constitutional amendment would not be worthy of its name. They banded together to form a separate organization, which immediately produced the Declaration of Goiânia, a strong statement in favor of sweeping structural reforms.[18]

The lines of battle formed around the issue of constitutional reform. Goulart, in the meantime, maintained a low profile. His first priority was the plebiscite, and until he achieved his aim, his behavior remained very circumspect and politically discreet. His speaking engagements included an appearance at the fourth Ruralist Conference on January 25, 1962, at which he assured the landowner membership of the Brazilian Rural Conferation that the purpose of a land reform could never be that of taking productive land away from owners and distributing it indiscriminantly to those who do not produce. "If anyone has the great social duty to give away land," the president reassured the fazendeiros, "that someone is the State."[19] Jango conceded that the constitutional provisions on expropriation might make land redistribution somewhat more difficult, but he was willing to accept that limitation. He informed his audience that he considered himself to be more conservative on the point of expropriation than even the Milton Campos commission, which was not renowned for its radical tendencies.

Goulart's low profile on agrarian matters carried over to his relations with the Congress as well. The Milton Campos commission finished its period of study and research, and submitted its moderate recommendations to the president. Campos himself introduced into the Senate an agrarian reform bill based on the work of his commission. Goulart had Prime Minister Tancredo Neves routinely present Congress with a request for a number of agrarian legislative measures. They included a bill on land rental, a bill to create an executive organization for agrarian reform, an amendment to return the land tax to federal jurisdiction, and one to alter the conditions for expropriation based on social need. In addition, the president endorsed the Rural Worker Law which had been introduced by Fernando Ferrari in 1961.

Oddly out of context, before the legislature adjourned, it passed a law establishing a Superindendency for Agrarian Reform, SUPRA, which was to replace the shorlived National Council on Agrarian Reform founded in February. The new agency regrouped already existing departments and possessed no additional independent financial or administrative resources. Its jurisdiction was unclear and there was no indication of how its parts were to be coordinated. Originally, SUPRA's creation had been recommended by the Special Commission on Agrarian Reform as an integral part of a comprehensive land reform program. The absence of such a program at this time and the nature of the new agency strengthened the impression that the measure was passed on the eve of the plebiscite primarily for political motives.

Responsible Government and the "Positive Left," January-June, 1963

The second phase of the Goulart administration began with the plebiscite of January 6, 1963, in which seven million votes were cast in favor of a return to the presidential system. Goulart, who had become president through succession, interpreted the vote as a personal mandate. He had the formal powers and hence the opportunity to demonstrate the seriousness of the commitments and promises he made throughout 1962. His attempt to live up to these commitments resulted in his experiment with the "positive left," a sector of center-left political opinion committed to fundamental change but based on realistic economics and moderation. San Tiago Dantas, whom the Congress had vetoed a year earlier as prime minister, became minister of finance and leader of the new cabinet which also included Celso Furtado as minister of planning and Almino Afonso, minister of labor, representing the radical left.

The new year started off on a seemingly serious, and responsible footing with the unveiling of the Three Year Plan of Economic and Social Development drawn up by Celso Furtado. Economic stablization and fiscal responsibility were important objectives, but they would not be achieved at the expense of fundamental reforms. The plan included provisions for tax, administrative, banking, and agrarian reforms.

The measures which Furtado advocated for agrarian development were moderately reformist, and tied integrally to the rest of his development plan. The specific measures included: 1) expansion of production relative to demand; 2) correction of distortions and deficiencies in the export crop sector; 3) increased productivity and improvement of the quality of primary products destined for the internal market; and 4) a position on land expropriation: "All lands considered necessary for the production of food, and which are not being used, or are being used for other purposes with yields inferior to the standards regionally established, could be expropriated according to our Plan, with long term payments."[20]

The land reform proposal actually forwarded by the president to Congress in March went well beyond the Furtado plan. It called for a constitutional amendment making it possible to pay for land expropriated by bonds, and proposed a program of forced leasing of unused lands. It also outlined a policy of technical and financial supports to agriculture (extension programs, credit facilities, colonization, and technical assistance) to complement the land distribution program.

Two aspects of this agrarian proposal make it seem that although he was still working on his alliance with the positive left, Jango was also getting ready to abandon it in favor of the "negative" left." First, as a part of the overall policy of conciliation and bridge building, the president formally entrusted his reform program to the PSD. This move appeared conciliatory but incongruous. The PSD was based primarily on rural political machines, represented some of the most traditional landed interests, and seemed an unlikely sponsor of reformist legislation. The Correio da Manhã speculated that perhaps Goulart did not really want reforms: "Amaral Peixoto, Benedito Valadares, Abelardo Jurema, and others. These men [known for their conservative politics and land based power] 'accepted' the stewardship of the reforms. Let's wait and see."[21] Goulart underscored his conciliatory stand by declaring at a cabinet meeting that he had no wish to interfere in the congressional debate on agrarian reform, since the national legislature should be able to deliberate freely, without pressure from the executive. In addition, he stressed that he did not wish in any manner "to strengthen the cause of those who wish the most radical reform."[22]

These overtures to the moderates were somewhat belied, however, by a second feature of the agrarian reform proposal. The draft of the constitutional amendment sent to the Chamber of Deputies stipulated that the maximum allowable correction for inflation on the land reform bonds would be ten percent. This meant that at a time when the rate of inflation had reached an all time high of eighty percent per year, the actual reimbursement would be a fraction of the stated value of the land at the time of expropriation. In addition, the amendment draft provided that the bonds would be paid out after the act of expropriation. As if this were not bad enough, in so far as the conservatives and some moderates were concerned, the land reform proposal carried a provision for the forced leasing of property. Goulart withdrew the last two provisions within two months. Nonetheless, this withdrawal, as much as the original presentation of the bill and amendment, were clear indications of political tactics rather than a commitment to economic or ideological purpose. They were also indications of an incipient change in the president's orientation toward a more radical, populist approach. In line with these inclinations, he severed all discussions, however informal, with landowners.

The tenuousness of Jango's solidarity with the positive left on land reform was accentuated by the activities of SUPRA. Following its creation by Congress late in 1962, it began to function in February, 1963, with João Caruso, who had been secretary of agriculture in Brizola's government in Rio Grande do Sul, as its first director. Caruso brought with him substantial experience in dealing with social issues of agriculture, organizing workers, and parcelling out land. Nevertheless, SUPRA activities during the first five months were limited. There was a minimal amount of expropriation, and some effort to establish professorships of rural sociology in agronomy schools -- an activity which to some conservatives smacked of radical political purpose.[23]

Generally, SUPRA was an administrative failure. Caruso complained there was no coherence to the institution, and no presidential interest or support for it. The heterogeneous executive council could not agree on the ground rules for functioning, and the director of the legal department, Fidelino Viana, was a dentist. Frustrated and outraged, Caruso attempted to resign in mid-June. In his letter to Goulart he stressed the lack of cooperation from other government departments:

> While your Excellency defends the necessity and urgency of reform, the Popular Agrarian Institutes retain the contributions they collect, which are destined for SUPRA's disposition. The Minister of Finance has not released a single cruzeiro, even from the budgetary allocation designed for the implementation of /rural/ services. Police sectors /of other government entities/ persecute landless agricultural workers and make it difficult for them to organize.[24]

Caruso was not able, however, to make his resignation immediately effective. He could not personally reach the president; the director of the legal department would not take over the responsibility for SUPRA; and the director of the Department of Rural Publicity and Organization, who might also have taken temporary charge, had not been seen for weeks.[25]

Caruso's difficulties in establishing reasonable administration within SUPRA reflected a change in the course of executive agrarian strategy. Concerned about losing the support of the leftist sections of the PTB and of organized labor and disillusioned by the failure of the Three Year plan to deliver to him the support of the center, Goulart abandoned the positive left. In a major cabinet reshuffle, he sacrificed Dantas and Furtado, as well as Almino Afonso and, in a gesture, seemed to rid himself of military, labor, and financial constraints. The new cabinet, however, did not inspire any confidence, in spite of the presence of the ex-governor of São Paulo, Carvalho Pinto as minister of finance. The weekly magazine, Visão, commented:

> We conclude that if the cabinet /reshuffle/ was intended to advance /socio-economic/ reforms, the effort backfired. If the objective was to bring the reform problem to an intentional impasse, the president succeeded, for he found the ideal scapegoat in congressional resistance. . . . Besides this cheap Machiavelianism there remains the plausible hypothesis that the president wishes to transform his role in the impasse into a /merely formal interest not backed by serious intentions/. . . ,[26]

-- But one, it might be added, which would enable him to continue capitalizing on the issue.

Populist Politics: End of Conciliation, June - December, 1963

Gloomily surveying the political scence, the Correio da Manhã produced the following mid-term assessment in an editorial aptly titled, "Portrait and Carricature:"

> This is the hour of the degeneration of technical problems into political debates, and of political debates into military issues. . . . The most conspicuous case is that of agrarian reform. The problem is technical. . . . but who mentions that?

> The politicians use agrarian reform as slogans of future presidential candidacies. With a total lack of knowledge and of ideas, some only wish to maintain the status quo at any price, and others, to destroy it, at any cost. Instead of sincere, reasonable discussion we hear weeping, bellows, shouts. And when all this is to no avail, they call on the sergeants to make an agrarian reform.[27]

Mildly prophetic, this statement captured some of the central political concerns of the second half of 1963. Personal political ambitions and rivalries increasingly diluted the substance of the agrarian issue. Agrarian reform became a vehicle for demagoguery and social disorder, a situation which the military watched with deepening concern. Apparently commited to a radical constituency which he could not control, Jango presided over increasing strikes, disorders, and demonstrations. The activities of Goulart's brother-in-law, Leonel Brizola, added to the general tension when he expropriated the American and Foreign Power Company in Rio Grande do Sul and encouraged rural unionization and land invasion. Inflation was skyrocketing, and economic activity was at an all time low. To make matters even worse, the poor harvests that had been foreseen months before were resulting in food shortages, hunger, and highly elevated prices for staples. On top of all this, charges of political corruption were rife, and a congressional investigation of election buying monopolized newspaper headlines.

The apparent victories of the radical left, consisting of salary increments and greater political mobilization, caused it to have an inflated perception of its own power and importance, and drove it to push more forcefully for a complete overhaul of society. The president, more captive than master of the radical surge, was swept along on the current, counting on reasonably good relations with the military to carry him through. In this both the extreme left and the president erred in their judgment. Even the legalists and constitutionalists among the military were becoming concerned about the social unrest, which was beginning to affect the enlisted men. Those politicians and military men who had been categorically opposed to Goulart's taking office began to gain new allies, now willing to consider ousting the president as a means of regaining political stability.

Political opposition to Goulart fed on the alienation generated by his increasingly desperate activities. Frustrated by his inability to get his programs enacted, in early October Jango called on Congress to give him decree powers for declaring a state of siege to intervene in Guanabara and São Paulo. He insisted plots were being hatched against him under the leadership of Governor Carlos Lacerda.[28] Jango reconsidered in the wake of strong public reaction within a few days, and the relieved Chamber unanimously approved the presidential message withdrawing the request for a state of siege.[29]

Despite the signs that opposition to him was increasing, Goulart did not abandon his radical tactics. Populist mass mobilization was not merely the basis of Goulart's political support; constant mobilization was his only available threat in bargaining with the opposition. Having maneuvered himself into an impasse, Goulart resorted to the threat of mass unrest and uprising as the only means of influencing the opposition to give in to his programs. With such a narrow constituency whose needs he had to satisfy at least on a symbolic level, Goulart had to stress incessantly and ever more dramatically his support for radical social legislation and economic and political reform. For this reason he finally turned to the strategy of popular agitation to promote agrarian reform, the focal point of his basic reform program.

SUPRA, under the direction of João Pinheiro Neto (briefly and unsuccessfully minister of labor in 1962) was ideally suited to this task. As Pinheiro admitted, SUPRA's objective situation had not changed in any way after the resignation of Caruso. There was still no land statute to implement, still no money, and still no plan. But in the eyes of the new director these were mere inconveniences. Promising to "crack this nut" of rural resistance he interpreted his primary task to be the generation of pressure in favor of radical agrarian reform, by whatever means possible.[30] SUPRA's activities until the end of the year centered on rural labor organization, speech-making, occasional expropriations, the organization of demonstrations, and generally whatever measures would increase rural agitation.[31]

Goulart complemented this strategy with another attempt to negotiate with Congress. Because of the division among the political elites and the impasse in which the presidency found itself Congress acquired an extraordinary importance during the Goulart term. This importance grew as Goulart's weakness and political predicament became increasingly apparent. The fact that Jango could not muster substantial political support outside the legislative arena, and that political and social groups were polarized and deadlocked over issues and over Goulart as well, contributed to the increasing Congress's political advantage. It was left to resolve, with a degree of power it did not normally possess, issues that no one else could or would. Its "increase" in power, was, in other words, a reflection of the immobility of other political groups and institutions. Since only Congress could grant Goulart the land reform he wanted, provided of course, the political rules of the game did not change, and since passage of agrarian reform was important for Goulart to legitimize him to the extreme left, he had no choice but to negotiate with Congress.

While continuing to support mass mobilization as a means to threaten his recalcitrant opposition, <u>within</u> Congress the president's approach became pragmatically conciliatory and his demands more moderate than they were in the first half of the year. He dissociated himself from his brother-in-law, Brizola, and from his radical policies, and actively worked for a conciliation of the PSD and PTB positions on the constitutional amendment. The apparent purpose of this strategy, which lasted through June and July was to prevent Chamber approval of the rival Milton Campos bill, which had passed the Senate in late 1962, and was now being considered by the lower house. If the bill were passed, it would destroy Goulart's chance of going down in history as the father of land reform in Brazil. On August 7, 1963 Goulart achieved this limited aim.

The Campos bill was defeated, but Goulart still had to secure congressional cooperation, particularly that of the Chamber, in order to have his own proposals passed. On this score he was not so fortunate. Following a lull of almost a month in the agrarian debate, several compromise formulas regarding the terms of land expropriation were considered. Goulart and the PSD leadership finally settled on a formula which, when officially made public in the beginning of September, proved unviable. First, the PSD representatives from Minas Gerais categorically refused to support any kind of constitutional amendment. Then, the compactos, the ideological wing of Goulart's own PTB, refused to accept the compromise package.

So far as the deputies were concerned, more was at issue than land reform. Both Goulart and the Congress knew that the president's legitimacy and credibility were intimately tied to the success of the reform measures. Also in play was the relative advantage of the political parties, as each one manipulated the agrarian issue to enhance its own political status both in Congress and in anticipation of the presidential election. The legislators soon determined that although social unrest was a serious concern, the executive did not possess an artillery of believable threats, and did not effectively control the situation. As a consequence Goulart did little to sway congressional opinion on land reform in his favor.

Frustrated by this stalemate, Goulart ceased to dialogue with the legislature. Briefly, at the end of September, there seemed some possibility that the president would abandon his withdrawn "contemplative attitude," and reestablish contact with Congress.[32] However, in October the original version of the Goulart-PTB amendment was brought to a vote and roundly defeated. From October, until Congress' adjournment in December, any remaining hope of securing a viable legislative agrarian package vanished. Thwarted in its attempt to gain congressional cooperation, the administration gave up any pretense of concern over political conciliation.

<u>Political Disintegration, December, 1963 - March, 1964</u>

If Goulart made any New Year's resolutions for 1964, one was apparently to abandon all efforts to work within the system. He left Congress to its own devices, and concentrated on securing his position on the radical populist front. In this final phase of his brief sojourn in the presidency the role of SUPRA became more important than ever. In particular, Pinheiro Neto caused grave concern in moderate and conservative political circles when SUPRA signed an agreement with the military. The ostensible objective of the agreement was to secure the help of the armed forces in cadastral surveying. It was becoming clear, however, that as the political impasse grew the military would exercise a more decisive political role in the months ahead. Thus, to Goulart's opposition it seemed as if SUPRA was succeeding only too well in establishing a base of military influence, and perhaps attempting to forestall unified military opposition to the government. Calling for more stringent criteria for the selection of administrative personnel, one deputy, incensed over Pinheiro Neto's behavior and policies, fumed:

> Only this way would we have the conviction that such a fundamental sector of state activity [as agriculture] has not been handed over to irresponsible professional agitators. We absolutely cannot entrust the gigantic task of Brazilian agrarian reform to office types, divorced from the rural reality, or to a playboy of cafe society whose nationalist decisions are stimulated by good doses of scotch whiskey in elegant salons or in the nightclubs of Copacabana.[33]

Oblivious to charges that his policies and tactics were divorced from reality, on March 13 Goulart signed two expropriation decrees, one affecting land, the other affecting private oil refineries. The land decree had originally been announced by Pinheiro in mid-December. At that time, it stipulated that the government would have the power to expropriate all land within thirty kilometers on each side of roads, wells, and dams. By the time the decree was signed, the limit was reduced to ten kilometers, a gesture which did little to sway the opposition in its determination that the time had come for Goulart to part with his office. The final spark for the revolution was provided when Jango provoked military insubordination among the rank and file by advocating a democratization of military procedure. He thus precipitated the wrath of the high command and his eviction from office.

In retrospect, Goulart's abortive efforts to promote land reform suffered from all the drawbacks of *ad hoc* policy. There was little planning, consistency, or coherence to balance the pursuit of short term populist political objectives. Jango was consequently left playing to a political theater empty of all but the radical galleries to which he repeatedly appealed. The credibility of his land reform program suffered as suspicions grew that his campaign for land reform was fueled by ulterior motives and devoid of a realistic assessment of the true needs and problems of Brazilian agriculture. In the view of the opposition, the mass mobilization and radical political rhetoric threatened not merely reform, but chaos. Appalled by the series of strikes, demonstrations, and land invasions, the conservatives were convinced these were a prelude to a radical personalist dictatorship. Goulart's attempt to secure decree powers in October 1963 certainly seemed to point in this direction.

Under these circumstances the passage of a truly redistributive agrarian reform within the political system operating in Brazil in the early 1960s would have been difficult, at best. Goulart's accession to the presidency made it altogether impossible.

CASTELO BRANCO AND LAND REFORM

The events of 1964 seem to mark a clear separation between two distinct eras in Brazilian politics. Preceding it was the populist democracy of the post-World War II period; and following, a military dictatorship combining strategies to promote economic growth with repressive social and political tactics.[34] Although the government of Castelo Branco unquestionably fell within the latter period and, in fact, inaugurated it, it nevertheless retained in some respects the characteristics of a transitional regime. The strain of maintaining a semblance of an open society eventually gave way under the pressures of economic austerity and political containment. During his first year and a half in office, however, Castelo made some attempt to preserve the appearance of civilian government. Primarily, he sought to convey the impression that he did not wish to redefine completely the constitution and the political system. Rather, his purpose was to provide a new sense of leadership, an elimination of destabilizing extremes of conduct and ideological expression, and a moral framework in which democracy could be made to function without threatening the basis of Brazil's political order. To this end, Castelo combined the exercise of expanded executive powers with observance of the formalities of the democratic process. In contrast to the later period of military rule, continuity with the pre-1964 regime was evident in the survival of the post-Vargas political party system, and in the continued functioning of governmental institutions, including the Congress. The government was a civilian-military enterprise, which dealt with political, economic and social problems in a decidedly more circumscribed context than that of the preceding regime, but one which still maintained elements of bargaining and competition.

This is not to say that the immediate impact of the Revolution was insubstantial. The radical "threat" collapsed like a house of cards in the face of censorship and a massive purge of leftist organizations and populist leadership. Thus, if the political club remained open for business, its membership was altered, and so, by implication, would be the decisions they arrived at. Furthermore, the rules of participation were also changed, with a significant effect on the character of policy formation. The first institutional act of April 9, 1964, besides increasing the powers of the executive and removing constitutional obstacles to a purge of the political leadership, altered the president's relationship to Congress. The 1946 constitution was formally retained, but the procedure by which Congress considered legislation was altered. The president acquired the right to initiate constitutional amendments, which could now be passed by a simple majority, instead of the two-thirds vote required previously. Also, Congress was required to act on both amendments and ordinary legislation within thirty days after the executive submitted the measure. Failure to do so would result in its automatic passage.[35]

Within this framework if the president were to pursue the enactment of a land reform law, he would still have to deal with Congress. However, the provisions of the Institutional Act affecting legislative procedure obviously gave Castelo an advantage not enjoyed by his immediate predecessors, although his powers were not as sweeping as those which were to be exercised by his successors.

The first revolutionary regime carried out an ambitious program of coordinated planning devised by a cabinet of dedicated technocrats under the leadership of Minister of Planning Roberto Campos. Both in his choice of cabinet ministers and in his policy preferences, Castelo was influenced by a group of thinkers from the National War College (*Escola Superior da Guerra* -- ESG) who, together with a small group of businessmen in Rio de Janeiro, had formed the Institute for Social Research and Study, IPES. Before April 1964, IPES considered political opposition to Goulart to be its first priority. Following the revolution, it provided, through its access to the president, personnel and policy statements and proposals that it had been working on for some period of time.[36] Under the leadership of planning minister Roberto Campos, the cabinet think tank produced a comprehensive program, the Government Program of Action (PAEG), which offered technocratic, capitalist solutions to Brazil's economic problems.[37] It proposed to reduce inflation, which in 1964 reached almost ninety percent, by means of austerity measures whose brunt would be felt principally by the lower class. Its scheme of economic rationalization sought to eliminate inefficient (and frequently traditional) aspects of the economy, introduce capitalism into traditional rural areas, stimulate private industry, and encourage foreign investment.

Among the many problems facing Brazil at this point, land reform was given a high priority, and Castelo made it clear that a land reform law was among his first objectives. Luís Viana Filho recalls that "in the first cabinet meeting of the new government, antagonizing the conservatives who had supported him, Castelo announced the agrarian reform urged by Roberto Campos."[38] There was no lack of documentation, studies, and proposals for land reform at this point. Not only was there a great collection of material from the work of the Milton Campos commission, but IPES as well had conducted a year-long study on the problem in 1963. At the end of that year, it produced a report and a series of proposals, which strongly resembled the Milton Campos bill.[39] Paulo Assis Ribeiro, who was primarily responsible for the project, continued to supervise it until it was finally enacted into law, accompanied by a constitutional amendment. This done, he became the first director of the new Brazilian Institute of Agrarian Reform (IBRA). The fact that Castelo insisted on the passage of a land reform law based on an amendment, and that he succeeded in his purpose within seven months of being in office is no small matter. No one had anticipated that as part of his program the new president would support two laws, one on land reform, and another on housing -- sensitive social issues which contributed so much to the fall of João Goulart.

Explanations for Castelo's desire to resolve the agrarian problem could be traced to his sophisticated awareness of the relation between economic and social problems and his first hand experience of rural problems as a native of the state of Ceará in the Northeast. His sensitivity to agrarian problems was no doubt reinforced by his participation in a seminar on agrarian problems at the Joaquim Nabuco Institute of Social Sciences, where he had the opportunity of exchanging ideas with sociologist Gilberto Freyre, Pernambuco governor Miguel Arrais, _ligas camponesas_ head Francisco Julião, and _camponês_ leaders and organizers Fathers Melo and Crespo.[40] Castelo's advisors openly acknowledged that the social unrest of the previous two years had made an impact on the first revolutionary president. In Castelo's view the urgency of an agrarian policy was mandated less by the grievances of Brazil's large rural population than by the fact that an effective agrarian policy was "a sure means of invigorating and stabilizing the entire national economy."[41] He therefore perceived land reform as a means of eliminating some of the causes for social unrest. Finally, in a situation where the masses, both rural and urban, would be particularly hard hit by the austerity program and by the political purge of all organizations tainted by association with Goulart, the agrarian and housing laws, passed in quick succession, were viewed as pacifiers.

The proposals, which remained largely unaltered as a result of discussions preceding their passage, consisted of a constitutional amendment, and an agrarian reform bill. Castelo's amendment (A-10) proposed to do what Jango could not accomplish: alter constitutional provisions affecting the expropriation of property. Like the Goulart-PTB proposal, the Castelo amendment would permit the payment for expropriated property to be made in bonds redeemable in twenty years. At variance with the earlier proposals, however, the new administration's measure insured a correction for inflation up to the full value of the bond. The value of the expropriated property would be equivalent to its taxable value.

Perhaps the most significant difference between the two amendments was the use to which each president intended to put it, reflecting distinct policy objectives. Jango intended to use the expropriation procedure made available by the amendment as a major instrument in promoting structural reforms. For him, the agrarian reform law was pointless without the amendment, and agricultural assistance provisions were an afterthought to a land policy focusing on the redistribution of property. Castelo, in contrast, perceived the amendment to be necessary as a means of providing flexibility and authority to an agrarian policy, but not as the central focus of that policy. Not expropriation, but progressive taxation constituted his major instrument of reform. The revolutionary government, unlike its predecessor, did not object to large properties -- only to large unused properties that could be brought under production, expropriated, or given over to agroindustry. Castelo's major objective, in other words, was not a redefinition of the social structure of rural areas, but productivity and agricultural development within a capitalist mode. The only social change in rural areas contemplated by the Land Statute of 1964 was the creation of a new group of middle class farmers.

Perhaps the most significant single element shared by the two presidents' agrarian policies was the conviction that the days of the traditional rural order were numbered. Their most significant disagreement reflected divergent perceptions of what the new order should be.

The Passage of the Land Statute

In the formulation of his agrarian policies, Castelo faced few immediate constraints. His position was not yet compromised by active competition among the military in preparation for the next presidential contest. Economic difficulties, because they were not yet compounded by politics, still appeared to be manageable, Congress had been purged of its leftist elements, including most of the leaders of the National Liberation Front, and the Institutional Act had facilitated the legislative process for the president. Within this framework, the agrarian policy initiatives of the president and the minister of planning proceeded smoothly, although not without opposition.

The agrarian policy process under Castelo differed from that under Goulart in more than formal institutional contraints. Jango's handling of the land reform debate was decentralized, and disjointed, devoid of any visible plan or long term strategy, accompanied by glaring publicity, and aimed primarily at winning the support of the masses while threatening conservatives generally, and landowners in particular. Also, it was singled out unabashedly as the keystone of a global attack on the entire political and social structure. Castelo, on the other hand, set into motion a process which was carefully planned and syncronized, controlled, subdued, with a minimum of media coverage. In contrast to Goulart's thorough neglect of the "producing classes," and as preparation for legislative approval of the agrarian policy proposal, Castelo and Campos deliberately and systematically included debates and discussions with the leadership of these groups. Campos, finance minister Bulhões, and agriculture minister Hugo Leme frequently commuted to São Paulo to assuage the fears of their most formidable opposition.[42] In any case, Castelo's proposals in no sense aimed to destroy the landowners or launch a frontal attack on the basis of their power. However, if Goulart overplayed publicity and general appeals to the public, Castelo did just the opposite, doing little to gain public understanding and support through explanatory statements. He expected his plans and their consequences to speak for themselves. This moratorium on publicity may have cost him some popular support. But it nevertheless served an important purpose in preventing a resurgence of panic on the part of the landowners.[43]

Despite the fact that Castelo concerned himself almost immediately with formulating an agrarian policy, the Congress did not interrupt its own activities with respect to this issue. During the months immediately preceding the revolution, at the point then the president abandoned any pretense of dialogue with the Congress, a group of deputies in the Chamber resolved to make another attempt to find a way out of their deadlock. The Campos bill had been defeated in the Chamber primarily because of its sponsorship by the UDN, rather than because of tis content. A number of the reformist PSD and UDN deputies in alliance with Christian Democrats and some other groups, reasoned that if a bill with a neutral sponsorship were to be introduced, it stood a good chance of securing some PTB support and therefore of passage. The enactment of an agrarian bill at this time was perceived as a means of preempting the possible implementation of Goulart's more radical designs. Accordingly, Christian Democrat Aniz Badra was induced to act as sponsor of the new bill, which appeared to be a more schematic, more poorly drafted version of the Campos bill. After the revolution, spurred by the threat implicit in Castelo's announcement of his own reform program, the Chamber passed the bill on April 7, 1964.

If passage of the bill by the Chamber was intended to forestall Castelo's presentation of his own land reform proposal, the strategy failed. In total disregard of what was already proposed or voted, the president introduced his own bill in the last days of April. Under the guidance of Paulo Assis Ribeiro, and in constant contact with Roberto Campos, the agrarian reform work group in the ministry of planning reviewed past legislation and drafted an agrarian reform bill heavily based on the IPES project drawn up earlier by Assis Ribeiro, which in turn relied on the Campos bill. The drafting of a constitutional amendment affecting the terms of expropriation was entrusted to Milton Campos following a similar process of discussion.[44] By the second week in May the proposal was ready for wider debate.

Unlike the previous regime, which lacked a defined plan of action, the Castelo government had mapped out a careful strategy for its proposal. The first step was to assuage the sore feelings of the landowners who not only had borne the brunt of the radical attack by the previous regime, but who had also cooperated in deposing it. Accordingly, the first consultation outside executive circles was with representatives of the Brazilian Rural Confederation (CRB).[45] The study group coordinator also met with a conference of the state agrarian federations. Concurrently, there were meetings with a representative of the Federation of Rural Workers of the State of São Paulo (FARESPE), of the National Union of Cooperatives, and with economists from the ministries of planning and agriculture.

The landowners' organization submitted a total of forty-four amendments to the proposal, of which forty were adopted. Members of both the CRB (in interviews) and of the administration seemed to agree that the changes accepted were not crucial, and that on all truly essential points, Roberto Campos, who made himself readily available to the CRB, remained aimable but steadfastly unmoved. Although the landowners, like other employer groups, did not have a decisive voice, the ruralists were pleased to be consulted and have their opinions taken into account and at least partially incorporated. The CRB was not, however, speaking for all the landowners -- a fact which explains subsequent landowner opposition to the measure. The staunchest defenders of the old order were not necessarily members of the confederation.

Following these preliminary consultations with the leadership of important social sectors and the approval of a new draft of the legislation by Roberto Campos, the bill was ready for limited circulation in a wider political circle as a restricted document. At this second stage, beginning the first of June, the circle of debate was widened to include Senate and Chamber leaders, the leadership of political parties, the Brazilian Rural Confederation, rural workers confederations, and state secretaries of agriculture. These consultations, made as a good will gesture by the government, did not have an appreciable impact on the bill. More influential was the president's personal review of the drafts of the bill and amendment. Further discussion with party leaders in Congress was delayed for the remainder of the month by petitions from paulista "producing classes," who requested further meetings with the work group and the president.

When the first of the meetings with congressional leaders was held on June 29, it became clear that congressional opposition, or more precisely, the UDN, (supposedly the government's "own" party) constituted the major obstacle to the passage of the amendment and law. The UDN leaders, including such social policy hard liners as Senator Daniel Krieger and Deputies Bilac Pinto and Ernani Sátiro, arrived with their own advisors, among them, Antônio Delfim Neto, who was to become minister of finance in 1967 under Costa e Silva and financial wizard of the revolution. The undenistas declared that they "considered the bill totally unacceptable for debate " and that they would "present their own substitute within thirty days."[46]

In comparison to the UDN, the PSD, with which the agrarian study group and Roberto Campos met next, seemed eminently more reasonable, maintaining an attitude of "constructive criticism," on both amendment and bill. The old politicians' party was, as usual, playing the accommodationist game. The PSD delegation, led by Amaral Peixoto, Gileno de Carli (who had drafted an agrarian bill of his own in 1962), and

Guilhermino de Oliveira, met several times with the group from July 2 to July 7.[47] Consultations with other parties followed. In none of these activities did the PTB appear to assume an important role.

Further discussions of the agrarian proposals were postponed for a short time awaiting the UDN substitute proposals. These never materialized. Concurrently, a meeting of state secretaries of agriculture in Viçosa, Minas Gerais from July 28 to 31 highlighted the agrarian issue and generated considerable publicity, while in substance affecting the proposal only marginally with suggested amendments and substitutes.[48] During August the bills underwent several more drafts. The tenth draft of the bill, which was submitted again for presidential perusal, reflected an important alteration. It no longer contained an amendment establishing a system of rural justice. The major veto apparently came from Milton Campos, then minister of justice, who adopted a decidedly conservative position in contrast to his sporting reformism during the Goulart period.[49]

During the subsequent slow waiting period, which dragged on into October, "educational" meetings on agrarian policy continued to be held. Roberto Campos devoted a great deal of time to addressing various groups, including what remained of rural unions in Recife. His activities also included lengthy sessions with the Chamber where the greater part of dissent and discussion was motivated by the still recalcitrant UDN leadership. The compromises exacted by the _undenistas_ in exchange for withdrawing their opposition appeared to include essential modifications on the location of taxing authority, on the final value of land reform bonds, and on the rate of the progressive taxation on idle land.[50]

The last week of October marked the final stage of the process of bringing a policy of land reform into being. On October 21, legislative consideration of the amendment was initiated in a special joint session required to reach a decision on the issue in thirty days. The land bill was submitted a few days later, on October 26. The careful and elaborate strategies pursued prior to the formal presentation of the measures to Congress no doubt aided considerably in smoothing the way to the acceptance of the bill, but by no means succeeded in eliminating all obstacles. Obviously prepared for this type of contingency, the minister of planning had his crew of consultants constantly on hand during the prolonged daily sessions until the measures had actually passed.

The major center of opposition was from the die-hard conservatives and the UDN in particular. The most conservative deputies expressed embittered outrage over what appeared to be a continuation of Goulart's policy. Others protested the impropriety of voting on the administration's measures while the Badra bill was presumably still under discussion. In the final days prior to the vote, the difficulties appeared to multiply rather than diminish. The UDN reporter of the special commission, Pacheco Chaves, resigned for reasons of total disagreement with the reformist measures. No ready substitute to fill his place could be found in either the UDN or the PSD. The government finally appealed to the "opposition" and convinced Senator Aurélio Viana, a member of the Brazilian Socialist Party, to undertake the responsibility of reporting on the measures to the joint session of Congress. In its review of the legislation and the 436 amendments submitted by the UDN, support for the agrarian task force came primarily -- and ironically -- from the opposition, i.e., the PTB, Christian Democrats, Socialists, and other minor parties, all of which had been heavily purged. However, as Goulart had discovered earlier, these votes alone were insufficient for the passage of the measures. Until the eve of the balloting the UDN leadership insisted on remaining in the opposition. At the last moment, however, following a meeting with the president, João Mendes urged the UDN legislators to vote as they individually saw fit. In the final analysis, it would appear that the party leaders felt it politically more expedient to contribute to having the national Congress pass the law than to see the legislation approved automatically as a result of congressional inaction. As a result, both Amendment No. 10, modifying articles 141 and 146, section 16 of the constitution and the Land Statute were passed by joint session of both houses of Congress. The amendment was approved on November 6, 1964. Only thirty-three deputies and two senators remained "guardians of democracy," as Deputy Último de Carvalho (PSD-Minas Gerais) put it with great sadness, and voted against it.

The Land Statute was destined to be the high point of land reform experience in Brazil. Several unique reasons explain the enactment of the reform measures at this time. First, President Castelo Branco accorded them top priority and his consistent and unequivocal personal support. Second, Institutional Act No. 1 have the executive ascendancy over Congress in the legislative process. Finally, despite some strong residual suspicions, the UDN and other anti-Goulart groups felt more secure about land reform in Castelo's hands than in those of his predecessor. Castelo's personal preoccupation with socio-economic reform was a luxury he could afford as long as the political, military, and economic problems did not become pressing. Shortly thereafter his attention became wholly absorbed by problems in his economic stabilization program. In the effort to impose economic stability, the niceties of social reform and democracy were pushed aside. If Castelo had not achieved the passage of the agrarian measures before 1965, he might not have been able to do so afterwards. As chapter 6 explains, the social impact of the legislation has in any case been minimal. Its enactment provided no automatic means of implementation and Castelo's successors have not shared his vision of social justice for the rural masses as a key to Brazil's economic stability.

NOTES

1. Needless to say, there were countless lesser proposals dealing with particular aspects of agriculture and with details of bills, as well as bills and decrees aimed at explaining and implementing previously discussed or enacted measures. A review of these measures would not contribute materially to understanding the agrarian debate.

2. Quadros, in his short time in office, left behind a record of concern for agriculure. In addition to creating a commision to study agrarian reform, he called into being an "Executive Coordinating Group for Rural Credit" and enhanced the availability of credit for agricultural production. JB, May 28, 1961, p. 11.

3. The new commission was composed of prominent national figures who were selected for their expertise in agricultural matters. The members of the Special Commission for Agrarian Reform were Milton Campos, UDN leader, statesman, former gover-

nor of Minas Gerais, and coordinator of the commission; Deputies Nestor Duarte and Barbosa Lima Sobrinho; Bishop Dom Fernando Gomez of Goiânia; Inâcio Rangel, Osvaldo Guzmão, and Jader Andrade of SUDENE, the Superintendancy for the Development of the Northeast; Rômulo de Almeida; Tomaz Pompeu de Accioly Borges, United Nations Food and Agricultural Organization (FAO); João Napoleao de Andrade, Brazilian Association of Rural Agricultural Credit, ABCAR; Ernani Maia and Ivã Luz, National Institute of Immigration and Colonization, INIC; Dom Helder Câmara, Bishop of Recife; and Edgar Teixeira Leite, of the Brazilian Rural Confederation, the landowners association. JB, May 20, 1961, 1/4, and August 15, 1961, 8/7,8. Also see Visão, April 28, 1961, p.14.

4. Osny Duarte Pereira, A Constituição Federal e Suas Modificações Incorporadas ao Texto (Rio de Janeiro: Civilização Brasileira, 1966).

5. ICOPS, Brazil Election Factbook (Washington, D.C.: Operations and Policy Research, 1965), p.84.

6. An absolute majority in each state assembly is required to merit approval. The proposal subsequently has to receive an absolute majority in two separate sessions (i.e., one year apart) in both houses, or a two-thirds majority in a single session in each house.

7. Ronald M. Schneider, The Political System of Brazil, pp. 83, 84. Even labor, which had been Goulart's primary constituency from the early fifties when he was made Vargas' minister of labor, was showing signs of independent behavior, calling into question Goulart's paternalistic assumptions in his relations with workers. Kenneth Erickson develops this point in his The Brazilian Corporative State and Working Class Politics.

8. Cf. Skidmore, pp. 266-267; Schneider, p.83.

9. Schneider, p.83.

10. Visão, February 17, 1961, p.13.

11. Ibid., February 24, 1961, p.15.

12. JB., December 31, 1961.

13. Politics in Brazil, p. 218.

14. Pernambuco had a territorial tax proposal before the state assembly in November 1961. JB, November 8, 1961, p.5.

15. Even the pretender to the nonexistent Brazilian throne, Prince João de Orleans e Bragança publicly endorsed a "balanced" land reform, but indicated strong disapproval of the "....demagogic activities of the ligas camponesas. JB, April 28, 1962, p.1.

16. Diario de São Paulo, May 2, 1961.

17. In its report on the meeting, Visão carried a photograph of the governors, with a caption that read, "Gathered in Araxá, the governors limited themselves to repeating what has already been said." June 15, 1962, p.18.

18. Among the signers were Arraes, Pernambuco; Ney Braga, Paraná; Brizola, Rio Grande do Sul; and Mauro Borges, Goiás.

19. Visão, February 2, 1962, p.13, and JB, January 26, 1962, p. 5.

20. Explanation by Furtado to Correio da Manhã, April 1, 1963, p. 1.

21. CM, March 22, 1963, p.6.

22. Ibid., May 19, 1963, p.6.

23. See, for instance, CM, June 13, 1963 on SUPRA expropriation of land in Paracambí and Campos in Rio de Janeiro state, and in the Vale do Rio Maranhão in Goias.

24. CM, June 14, 1963, Canderno 2, p.1.

25. CM, June 18, 1963, p.3.

26. Visão, June 28, 1963.

27. May 12, 1963, p.6. This last is a reference to the appeal made by Brizola to the military of Natal the preceding week.

28. Ibid., October 5, 1963, p.1. As it turned out, in the long run he was not entirely mistaken. The two cities played an important part in coordinating the opposition movement which eventually deposed him.

29. CM, October 8, 1963, p.1.

30. Ibid., August 17, 1963, p.2; July 10, 1963, p.10; June 28, 1963, p.2.

31. There is a resemblance between SUPRA, and its Chilean counterpart, INDAP. INDAP, under the direction of Jacques

Chonchol, was charged with communist infiltration and deliberate agitation in the countryside. Cf., Robert Kaufman, The Politics of Land Reform in Chile, 1950-1970. Public Policy, Political Institutions, and Social Change (Cambridge, Massachusetts: Harvard University Press, 1972), pp. 102-103.

32. CM, September 25, 1963, p.6.

33. Anais da Câmara, I, 1963/1964, 12 session, January 12, 1964. Cited hereafter as Anais.

34. For a review of this period see Schneider, The Political System of Brazil; Luís Viana Filho, O Govêrno Castelo Branco (Rio de Janeiro: Livraria José Olympio, 1975); Riordan Roett, editor, Brazil in the Sixties (Nashville, Tenn.: Vanderbilt University Press, 1972); Alfred Stepan, editor, Authoritarian Brazil (New Haven: Yale University Press, 1973); and Georges-André Fiechter, Brazil since 1964: Modernization Under a Military Regime (New York: John Wiley, 1975).

35. A complete compilation of the 1946 constitution, with all amendments, institutional acts and complimentary acts up to 1966 can be found in Osny Duarte Pereira, A Constituição Federal e suas Modificações Incorporadas ao Texto (Rio de Janeiro: Civilização Brasileira, 1966).

36. Affiliates of IPES who found their way into the service of the Castelo government included: Roberto Campos, Minister of Planning; Octavio Bulhões, Minister of Finance; Luís Viana Filho, Chief of the Civilian Household; Garrido Tôrres, Director of the National Institute of Economic Development; General Golbery de Couto e Silva, Director of the National Information (security) Service. Source: IPES files.

37. On the economic policies of the military government see Albert Fishlow, "Some Reflections on Post-1964 Brazilian Economic Policy," in Stepan; Ministério do Planejamento e Coordenação Econômica, Programa de Ação Econômica do Govêrno, 1964-1966 (Rio de Janeiro, 1964); Celso Furtado, Análise do Modelo Brasileiro (Rio de Janeiro: Civilização Brasileira, 1972); and Mário Enrique Simonsen, A Nôva Economia Brasileira (Rio de Janeiro: Livraria José Olympio, 1974).

38. O Govêrno Castelo Branco, p. 274.

39. The report was published in 1964 as: A Reforma Agrária: Problemas, Bases, e Soluções.

40. Viana Filho, p. 274.

41. Ibid., p. 262.

42. Ibid., pp. 263, 264.

43. Congressional debates, newspapers, and journals, which had been excellent sources for the reconstruction of the land reform debate under Goulart were poor sources on this issue after April 164, both because of the absence of publicity by the government and increased repression and censorship. Besides relying, where possible, on these standard sources, I have reconstructed the passage of the Land Statute from numerous interviews conducted with persons directly involved -- politicians, cabinet ministers, and administrators -- and from a particularly useful report written by Paulo Assis Ribeiro describing in minute detail the passage of Amendment No. 10 and of the Land Statute: "Implantação da Reforma Agrária. Relatôrio de Abril 1964 -- Março 1967," (Rio de Janeiro, 1967, mimeo). Luís Viana Filho's chapter on agrarian policy in his book on the Castelo government is a somewhat superficial treatment of the subject. It offers a few otherwise unpublished details of the period based on personal correspondence and observation from his vantage point as Chief of the Civilian Household. Its treatment of the struggle over issues is unfortunately uninformative.

44. Ibid., p. 276.

45. Particularly with Eudes de Souza Leão Pinto, José Resende Peres, Durval Garcia de Menezes, and Edgar Teixeira Leite.

46. Assis Ribeiro, "Implantação," p.3.

47. Ibid.

48. Ibid., p.4.

49. Ibid., p.6.

50. Ibid., p.7.

4. The Congressional Debate: Legislative Politics and the Policy Process

Historically, Latin American legislatures have neither enjoyed stability of existence nor consistency of institutional integrity. Whenever they have attempted decisive structural reforms of their nations' social and economic systems, powerful conservative elites have repeatedly conspired to overturn them in favor of centralized authoritarian rule. During the periods when it has been in existence, the Brazilian Congress has generally been considered more powerful than those of its Spanish speaking neighbors. It too, however, has been subject to periodic subordination and suspension by authoritarian regimes. In the course of those highly centralized intervals, when the Congress has functioned at all, such as during the Vargas dictatorship and the present military government, it has been reduced to a rubber stamp.

Because of the persistence of regional power, the Brazilian Congress has had the ability to reassert itself. Regional interests have historically found most prominent expression in the Congress and in a functioning federal system. The Old Republic (1889-1930), dominated by the "politics of the governors," and the Second Republic (1946-1964) were characterized by strong state and regional political influence. Some of the major efforts of both the Vargas dictatorship and the present military regime have, in fact, concentrated on curbing the independent political expression found at the state level and manifested in the Congress.

In addition to providing a direct avenue of expression for regional interests, the Brazilian legislature has also served another important purpose. With the expansion of suffrage in the twentieth century it has functioned as an arena for the expression of newly mobilized political groups. The politics of mass mobilization created opportunities for populist political leaders to organize new constituencies as a basis for political careerism. Although these political actors more often than not represented their own interests rather than the interests of their constituencies, they nevertheless promoted popular reformist issues as a means of creating a broader base of power. Thus, a politics of symbolism rather than substance came to dominate congressional behavior.

A careful examination of congressional behavior in reference to the highly charged land reform issue can yield some valuable insights into how various elements of the Brazilian political system responded to the threat of basic social reform. Particularly during the unrestrained "democratic" period of Goulart, an examination of congressional activity reveals the full spectrum of ideological and institutional conflict over basic reforms. Since the legislature is an official forum, the attitudes and strategies of political parties and groups remain a matter of public record to a greater extent than in the absence of legislative activity. This permits a more careful scrutiny than might otherwise be possible of attitudes expressed and positions taken on a given issue.

The fact that the land reform issue spans two political periods divided by the 1964 revolution permits the study of the influence of the Congress under distinct circumstances. Clearly, the survival of some congressional independence into the Castelo period enhances the comparability of congressional activity under the two regimes. Political party behavior and attitudes can thus be traced and compared for programmatic and ideological consistency or, by contrast, for political opportunism.

Finally, legislative behavior can be assessed in relation to more immediate political circumstances and, most particularly, in terms of the conduct of the presidency and the degree of consensus among national elites. Weakness or indecision on the part of the executive has invariably resulted in an increase of congressional leverage. Precisely this type of situation prevailed under João Goulart. He assumed power in the midst of a crisis and in the face of considerable political and military opposition. His subsequent need to rely on left wing populism in the absence of firm support from the military and major economic and social interests only aggravated his problems. During the Goulart administration, executive power was circumscribed not only by the formal institutional arrangements of representative democracy, but also by immediate political circumstances. The land reform issue thus provides an opportunity to examine congressional behavior, if not at its best, at least at its strongest.

The Castelo period, in contrast, is characterized by a decidedly more unified elite and also by an executive who, whatever his popularity, enjoyed considerable respect, and the crucial support of strategic economic and political elites. For these as well as institutional reasons, the scope of congressional activity was more limited.

The following examination of the Brazilian Congress is divided into two parts. This chapter will detail the struggle between the president and Congress over agrarian policy from the point of view of the latter. The next chapter will take a closer look at the behavior of legislators for the purpose of analyzing the interaction of ideology, interests, and opportunism in political behavior.

As noted earlier, bills introduced by the president must first be considered by the Chamber of Deputies. If approved by the lower house, they are brought before the Senate. Since Goulart's agrarian proposals never reached this point, the Chamber will be the major focus of this discussion.

POLITICAL PARTIES AND INTEREST REPRESENTATION

The political party system which functioned until 1965, and which continues to exist under the cover of the present two official parties, came into being in 1945 when Getúlio Vargas stepped down from power after a fifteen year sojourn in the presidency. Three major parties, as well as a number of small ones, came into existence. Of the larger ones, the National Democratic Union, UDN, had brought together the opposition to Vargas, and was based on a heterogeneous coalition of social groups The other two major parties, the Social Democratic Party, PSD, and the Brazilian Labor Party, PTB, were both created by

Table 4-1

BRAZILIAN POLITICAL PARTIES, 1945-1964

Political Party	Initials	Translation
Partido de Representação Popular	PRP	Popular Representation Party
Partido Republicano	PR	Republican Party
Partido Social Progressista	PSP	Social Progressive Party
Partido Liberal	PL	Liberal Party
União Democrática Nacional	UDN	National Democratic Union
Partido Social Democrático	PSD	Social Democratic Party
Partido Democrata Cristão	PDC	Christian Democratic Party
Partido Trabalhista Brasileiro	PTB	Brazilian Labor Party
Partido Trabalhista Nacional	PTN	National Labor Party
Partido Social Trabalhista	PST	Social Labor Party
Partido Socialista Brasileiro	PSB	Brazilian Socialist Party
Partido Comunista Brasileiro*	PCB	Brazilian Communist Party
Movimento Trabalhista Renovador	MTR	Labor Renovation Movement
Partido Ruralista Brasileiro**	PRB	Brazilian Ruralist Party
Partido Orientador Trabalhista**	POT	Orienting Labor Party
Partido de Boa Vontade	PBV	Good Will Party

* Illegal as of 1948

** Cancelled following 1950 elections because of insufficient votes.

Vargas himself. The origins of the PTB can be traced back to the Estado Nôvo phase of the Vargas dictatorship, when labor was organized to serve as a personal vehicle for the president. The PSD was formed out of the state political machines that had functioned during the old Republic, and on which Vargas built his government. Essentially a "politicians party,"[1] it was an organization of political in-groups, whose primary interest was that of maintaining themselves in office.

Of all the parties, only the PSD, PTB, and UDN enjoyed a nation-wide base, which in no way implied ideological consistency or programmatic uniformity. The primary attraction these parties held out for the electorate was that of personalities rather than principles. Ideological and programmatic inconsistency was manifest in indiscriminate alliances and the irrelevance of party platforms to the character and interests of constituencies. State sections of a party frequently found themselves contradicting each other as well as the national leadership. Parties allied at the national level or in one state could be in bitter opposition in another.

Since the primary functions of the party system were political control and elite recruitment, not representation, these characteristics might not have been a serious shortcoming from a system maintenance point of view. Indeed the clientelistic-patrimonial relationship of politicians to the electorate on one hand, and the emotional and vaguely nationalistic populism on the other are perfectly logical from this perspective.

However expedient, this system bore the seeds of its own destruction. The growing electorate --

particularly in urban areas -- generated a race among parties for new constituencies. In the long run, the concurrent strategies of mass mobilization to create new electoral constituencies, and elite control to contain the latter's reformist expectations were contradictory and created tensions in the functioning of the political system. The political system was unable to absorb successfully the rapid social mobilization that had taken place. Thus it was becoming clear that populism was getting out of hand and beginning to threaten the stability of clientelism as a control mechanism. This is particularly evident in the distribution of seats by party in the two houses of Congress. Table 4-2 indicates that in the 1945 to 1964 period, two important changes occurred. First, among the three major parties, the net balance shifted from the traditional and clientelistically based PSD and UDN and toward the more populistically inclined PTB in both houses of Congress. Second, although the three major parties managed to retain a constant percentage of the seats in the Senate, their combined share in the Chamber of Deputies dropped 10.4 percent.

The gains of the PTB and the minor parties signaled a threat to the clientelistic basis of politics in Brazil and to elite control. The accession of Goulart to the presidency dramatically emphasized the dangers of this process to the strategic elites. Deprived of their support, Goulart relied almost exclusively on an increasingly radical populist strategy. To make matters worse, as a result of six deputies switching parties, the PTB in 1963 became the majority party in the Chamber for the first time, casting it in a leadership role in the lower house,

Table 4-2

DISTRIBUTION OF CONGRESSIONAL SEATS BY PARTY, 1954-1960

		1945	%	1950	%	1955	%	1960	%	% Net shift
Senate:	total seats	42	100	63	100	63	100	63	100	
	PSD	26	61.9	28	44.4	23	36.5	21	33.3	-28.6
	UDN	10	23.8	11	17.5	13	20.6	19	30.2	+ 6.4
	PTB	2	4.8	5	7.9	16	25.4	17	27.0	+22.2
	3 major parties	38	90.5	44	69.8	52	82.5	57	90.5	0
	Others	4	9.5	19	30.2	11	17.5	6	9.5	0
Chamber:	total seats	286	100	304	100	326	100	326	100	
	PSD	151	52.8	93	30.6	114	35.0	115	35.3	-17.5
	UDN	77	26.9	54	17.8	74	22.7	70	21.5	- 5.4
	PTB	22	7.7	43	14.1	56	17.2	66	20.2	+12.5
	3 major parties	250	87.4	190	62.5	244	74.9	251	23.0	-64.4
	Others	36	12.6	114	37.5	82	25.1	75	77.0	+64.4

Source: Adaptation of Table 5 in Marta Cehelsky, "A Case Study in Urbanization: Brazil" in Philip B. Taylor and Sam Schulman, eds. Population and Urbanization Problems in Latin America, University of Houston, 1971, p.68.

and giving it greater leverage over committee business. The populist trend gave credence to the fears of conservatives that political stability was about to be engulfed by a populist wave.

Curiously, the actual effect of populism on Brazilian politics was somewhat ambiguous. Populism did succeed in mobilizing more people into the political arena and at a greater rate than the elistist and statist political system could absorb without endangering its stability. Thus, from their perspective, conservative elites may have been correct in fearing this phenomenon's potential for the prevailing social order. Their perceptions, however, of the ideological importance of the threat were misplaced. Populism was ideologically oriented only presumptively and indirectly by serving as a political procedure for the incorporation of the masses. Since the masses and the issues of their oppression and rights were consistently identified with radical leftist programs, the ideological inference was easy to make. In actual fact, however, although vaguely nationalistic and reformist, populism was not particularly more expressive of ideologies and interests than was clientelism. Acting as often to obfuscate as to clarify issues and interests, neither populism nor clientelism served as effective vehicles for the articulation of competing class and group demands. Consequently, Brazilian elections mobilized the electorate without producing outcomes which significantly discriminated among specific group needs and interests according to party ideology.

A possible alternative route for interest expression bypassing the electoral process might have been the use of lobbies and pressure groups to influence legislators directly. In fact, my analysis of the land reform issue indicates that social and economic organizations in Brazil are poor articulators or interests, especially before Congress.[2] The corporatist and clientelistic organization of social and economic groups causes its members to direct the bulk of their attention to the executive, who can be counted on to deliver the desired pay offs. In his study of interest group behavior in Brazil, Schmitter observes that to the extent that an interest group focuses on the Congress, its target is more likely to be an individual congressman with whom, presumably, a preexisting clientelistic relationship obtains rather than the objective working commission which reviews pending legislation. Group activity might in this sense be described as being generally person oriented rather than issue oriented. This observation is borne out in my study of the discussion of land reform. Groups concerned with this issue would send letters, messages, and telegrams to individual deputies. These, in turn, would read the communications into the legislative record and consider their obligation fulfilled. Congressmen do not, with some exceptions, see themselves as representatives of specific interests.

Until the early sixties, individual appeals constituted the full extent of pressure activity by economic interests in Congress. Then, at least to a limited degree, a more organized attempt at pressure group activity became apparent. Two highly organized pressure groups came into being with heavy industrial financial backing, as well as support from foreign business firms. The first of these groups, the

Brazilian Institute for Democratic Action, IBAD, was founded in 1959 for the declared purpose of "defending democracy."[3] The other organization, the Institute of Social Research and Study, IPES, came into being in 1962, also supported by industry and a sector of the military. Its obstensible purpose was to study national problems and their relationship to democratic principles.[4] Both groups claimed to have been inspired by the Alliance for Progress and the encyclicals of Pope John XXIII.

Well publicized congressional investigations of the two organizations revealed that altruism was perhaps not the main motivation for IPES and IBAD, and that their activities were not politically innocuous. IBAD was charged with "tampering with elections, and corruption of the press, politicians, and authorities through internal and external resources."[5] Although the congressional investigation could not actually prove that IPES was guilty of similar activities, there is evidence that suggests this organization was no less innocent of such charges.[6]

Of greater interest is the decision made by these two organizations to establish themselves in the Chamber of Deputies with consultants, aids, microphones, telephones, and a working budget. Of the two organizations, IPES seems to have been more active and also more directly responsible for the tasks of buttonholing legislators, and lining up support for IPES sponsored bills.[7] By March 1963, IPES had submitted 24 bills through "its" deputies.

Although it cannot be said that IPES ever acquired anything approaching a controlling influence in the Chamber, it at least enjoyed close ties with such leaders of the conservative democratic Parliamentary Action bloc in the lower house as João Mendes and Raymundo Padilha. Another aspect of its special leverage in Congress originated in its research functions. IPES systematically concerned itself with the preparation of studies on major issues under consideration by the president and Congress. Among its most important studies was that of agrarian reform. Although it failed to have a bill of its own introduced in the legislature, its agrarian reform study ultimately served as a working document for the elaboration of the Land Statute.

LEGISLATING LAND REFORM: JOÃO GOULART

That an institutional crisis was at the heart of the debate on structural reforms seemed fairly clear to members of the politically aware public. Visão cogently pointed out that this crisis could be traced at least to Jânio Quadros' resignation in 1962. The leadership vacuum, the article noted, had not been filled since then, with a resulting absence of adequate authority to confront critical decisions.

> In political epoques such as ours, there is no one with this authority and this power. It is pointless to speak of coherent economic policy when the major political and economic problem, the issue of income redistribution. . . , is not conducted with real authority [derived from] free consent from below. . . . The left, as much as the right, has no faith in the efficacy of the Brazilian political class. . . .[8]

João Goulart himself was particularly anxious to resolve this crisis of immobility, not the least for his own sake. Congress too was beginning to feel the pressure of public opprobrium. Typically, the media lamented that at a time when the country was in desperate need of a variety of reform measures, the national legislature contented itself with being nothing more than "a simple machine for obtaining favors."[9] Newspapers admonished the national legislators that Congress would be left behind, obsolete and disgraced, as the rest of the nation, with the President in the lead, embarked on an ambitious program of social reforms. These reproaches seems finally to affect some of the legislators. In a typical remark, a Deputy from Pernambuco declared that "instead of discussing the gender of angels and the allocation of minor posts," Congress ought to get to work considering such substantive policy proposals as agrarian reform.[10]

It seemed fairly clear to most national legislators that the time was fast approaching when some sort of agrarian legislation would be passed. The real bone of contention and the point that was to cause polarization and heated argument were the pivotal issues of what really constituted land reform and how it was to be carried out. Those who were arguing for land reform, in the root meaning of the term, insisted that only a total revision of the land tenure system through expropriation of latifundia and redistribution to the landless or to minifundia owners could solve the social and economic problems of the countryside. But such a program of expropriation would ultimately require that the constitution be amended to permit expropriation of land and payment for it in bonds redeemable after a number of years had elapsed. Consequently, to these partisans, the cause of the agrarian controversy could be reduced to the problem of the constitutional amendment. But the issue was much more complex than just a simple choice between altering the constitution, or retaining the standing provisions requiring prior payment in cash for expropriated land. There were several subsidiary issues, such as the degree of correction for inflation to be permitted in the case of agrarian bonds; the definition of a latifundium; the specification of which level of government would have powers to tax the land (_município_, state government, or federal government); and the rate of taxation on unproductive land.

Other dilemmas surfaced to further complicate the issue. Ideological positions were by no means the only stakes in the debate. Of no small consequence was the challenge to the president's legitimacy to govern and establish policy. Similarly at issue were the positions and careers of a number of deputies whose power base lay in the countryside. At another level of consideration there was the strategic problem of relative gains. Each party, and each deputy, when asked to consider a presidential proposal, addressed not only the objective merits of the measure, but also its political and electoral consequences. The progress and success of political careers depended on tactical victories that would increase access to clientolistic payoffs or enhance the position of a given political actor or group in the populist struggle at the polls. Thus, presidential candidates and party factions fastened on agrarian reform as an issue with high visibility and good potential for enhancing their own positions. It was the president's task to forge out of this material a block of alliances capable of furnishing the support he needed for his own political goals.

Phase I: Agrarian Policy and Congressional Strategies

For the legislature and for political parties, as for the president, the parlimentary experiment of 1962 was a period of indecision, a time of taking stock, and in general, the calm before the storm. The formal limitations of parliamentary government made any interaction between the executive and legislative branches unfruitful for the resolution of problems. There was general dissatisfaction with the current institutional arrangement, and an uncertainty fed by the knowledge that they would be revised by a plebiscite at some point in the near future. Consequently, the foremost political concerns of all politicians were the plebiscite on the one hand, and on the other, the congressional elections of October 1962 which would determine the party balance in Congress with which Goulart would deal for most of his term.

As pointed out earlier in the discussion of presidential policy, Goulart's strategy for this period was to do everything in his power to ensure an early plebiscite. For this reason, his public statements and political tactics were deliberately restrained, and leaned toward conservatism. Presumably to make himself as non-controversial as possible to political moderates and conservatives the president did not become centrally involved in the October elections. He had already presented his plan of Basic Reforms (agrarian, tax, administrative, fiscal, educational reforms) to the country, but was careful not to appear too radical or too insistent.

Congress and the political parties were facing a somewhat different set of problems in regard to basic reforms. If Goulart's need was to tone down a radical image, that of Congress, or more particularly of the two large conservative parties, the UDN and the PSD, was to live down the accusations made in the press that their immobilism was responsible for the social turmoil and policy impasse. Their strategy was to come out clearly in favor of structural reforms in a series of declarations made from late 1961 through mid-1962.

The objective reasons for the pro-reform unanimity were easily apparent. Some sort of national policy would, it was expected, bring under control the radicalizing tendencies spontaneously appearing in the countryside: _ligas camponesas_ led by a man clearly sympathetic to the views of Fidel Castro; rural unions organized by the Catholic church, and by the Communist Party; land invasions; and even attempts by individual states to deal with agrarian problems in moderate (São Paulo under Carvalho Pinto) or radical (Rio Grande do Sul under Brizola) fashion.

But there were other reasons as well. It was easy enough for congressmen and their parties to be in favor of "reforms" when they were innocuous, or when their exact provisions were not spelled out. In such circumstances a pro-reform position could only enhance one's political appeal. It was another matter to approve a series of specific proposals potentially threatening to one's political career or contrary to one's political principles. A good case in point is that of the UDN. When Quadros resigned, the National Democratic Union, whose candidate he had been, announced that it continued to support the programs of structural reforms that had been called for by the ex-president. Magalhães Pinto, governor of the state of Minas Gerais and leader of the party at the time, declared in October 1961 that if land reform and other structural and social reforms were delayed, Brazil would find itself in danger of massive social upheaval.[11] He counseled the nation to put into effect the reformist promises that Jânio had made. Senator Milton Campos, who had presided over the former president's Special Commission for Agrarian Reform, introduced a moderate land reform bill into the Senate in August 1961. The UDN apparently felt that so long as the reformist initiative was in its own hands reformist policy would remain nonthreatening. The party leadership therefore fostered the Campos bill through the Senate to a favorable vote at the end of 1962. In the meantime, the party evidently felt safe enough behind the protection of the parliamentary system and the constitutional change which had put land taxation in the hands of <u>municípios</u>, to publicly endorse President Goulart's statement in favor of basic reforms in June of the same year.[12]

Within a month of Congress' reconvening in March of 1963, however, the UDN position changed radically. Two divisive issues had arisen to provoke a fight within party ranks leading to the ultimate triumph of the anti-reform faction. The first issue was that of the president's insistence, by way of his prime minister's speech to Congress in August 1962, that it was absolutely necessary that the national legislature pass a land reform law accompanied by an amendment to the constitution changing the provisions affecting expropriation of land. An important segment of UDN opinion viewed such a proposition with discomfort, if not alarm, and felt that the UDN should go on record as categorically opposed to any such constitutional change, especially now that Goulart was invested with full presidential powers. The second issue was one of party control and presidential aspiration. The UDN pro-reform position had been articulated by party leader Magalhães Pinto. Carlos Lacerda, governor of Guanabara, and the single most dedicated opponent of Vargas and all his allies and heirs (Goulart was one of the latter), was determined to wrest UDN control from Magalhães Pinto. The two issues converged at the UDN convention in Curitíba in the state of Paraná at the end of April 1963. Lacerda presented the UDN leadership with an ultimatum. Either the UDN would clearly oppose any land reform proposal that was accompanied by a constitutional amendment, or he would retire from politics. Apparently, the prospect of being abandoned by the powerful UDN founding father when elections were looming on the horizon was too frightening. Anti-reform feeling within the party triumphed and a surprisingly strong majority voted against sweeping structural reforms and for Lacerda.[13]

Not all _udenistas_ agreed with the party decision. A small group of reformists within the UDN, who called themselves the "_bossa nova_," argued that social conditions dictated the need for sweeping reforms, including modification of the constitution, and that the UDN must come out clearly in support for such reforms or be left behind. Repudiating the _Carta de Princípios_ (letter of principles) issued at Curitiba, the group publicly endorsed a strong pro-structural reform position, including land reform based on amendment.[14] The _bossa nova_, however, was a small splinter group, and could not hope to turn around the vast bulk of the party. Nevertheless, its failure to conform to the stated party position did act as a thorn in the side of the party leadership.[15]

The PSD also underwent a process of reassessment from 1961 to early 1963. Its position, however, differed from that of the UDN. There was no doubt about the latter's opposition role to the PTB oriented government in power. Nor could the UDN pretend to exercise political leadership in the Congress since it was not the majority party in either of the two houses. By contrast, the PSD was the majority party in the Chamber of Deputies. The utility of reaching an understanding with the executive was dictacted by this and other good reasons. Prominent among them was the party's pragmatic, accommodationist inclination, as exemplified by its practice of entering alliances with the other Vargas-founded party, PTB; its habit of being in power and willingness to subordinate principle to political gain;[16] and, finally, the eagerness of the PSD leadership to take advantage of the populist payoff on the land reform issue. As a result, party head Amaral Peixoto (Vargas' son-in-law) announced in a formal statement from Brasília that the PSD was solidly behind reforms in general both because they were just and because they would act to control any revolutionary stirrings in the countryside. The PSD would urge its membership in the Congress to take positive action on two agrarian proposals that had been submitted by PSD deputies Gileno de Carli and José Joffily.[17] Ex-President Juscelino Kubitschek, who was already campaigning for his second presidential term, warned that it would be an "unspeakable crime" not to effect immediately a sweeping reform program which would even include a provision for enfranchising illiterate people.[18]

The bandwagon approach to dealing with the administration's proposals generated opposition within PSD ranks. The tension mounted between its essentially conservative landowning constituency, and the party's leadership over the latter's desire for electoral reasons to keep apace of reformist policies of the government. This caused the PSD to engage in the never ending pursuit of an ideal compromise. By April 1962, the necessity to come to terms with its staunchly conservative and powerful faction from Minas Gerais caused the PSD to modify its reformist posture to the point that the _Carta de Brasília_ (letter of Brasilia) which it produced that month strongly resembled the _Carta de Princípios_ drafted by the UDN under Lacerda's direction. Its former five-point program on land reform, which had taken a favorable stand on the issue of constitutional reform, was pared down to a single vague sentence.[22] Amaral Peixoto justified these changes in the PSD position by arguing that, in fact, the party still supported land reform and the amendment proposal, but that it was pointless to make broad commitments without reference to specific legislation. After all, not all land reform bills called for expropriation of land payable in bonds.[20] By no means was this to be the _pessedista's_ final statement on the issue.

The third major party, the Brazilian Labor Party (PTB), conformed to the strategy defined by its major leader, President João Goulart. It was already clear in 1962, however, that the radical wing of the party under Brizola's leadership was gaining strength and might be expected to behave less than docily towards the president's political scheming the following year.

The jockeying of the parties in Congress generated no conclusive results in 1962. Everyone, the president included, wished at that point to appear strongly and seriously pro-land reform without necessarily doing anything about it. Jango's Basic Reforms proposal was discussed alongside of other measures introduced by deputies and senators, but no major decisions were made. The president of the Chamber, Ranieri Mazilli, informed the prime minister in October that it was most unrealistic to expect any vote on agrarian reform that year. Too much else was on the agenda. In addition, the impending congressional elections were bound to absorb everyone's attention for what remained of that congressional session.[21] One deputy observed cryptically that the intensity and frequency of the inconclusive discussions on land reform were related directly to the election campaign, as could be seen from the precipitous drop in interest in the issue immediately after the elction.[22] It was not an entirely unproductive year in terms of rural benefits, however. For one thing, Congress approved the creation of SUPRA (Superintendency for Agrarian Reform). For another, the Chamber had approved, and sent to the Senate, the bill for the Rural Worker Statute calculated to extend to rural workers the rights and protection enjoyed by urban workers since the Vargas period. Finally, the Senate passed the Milton Campos bill and forwarded it to the Chamber.

Phase II: The Politics of Conciliation: Frustration and Disillusionment

Negotiation. When Congress reconvened in March 1963, the lines of battle were fairly clearly drawn. As anticipated, the presidential message to Congress, which presented the Three Year Plan drawn up by Celso Furtado as part of Goulart's positive left experiment, contained a strong statement on the urgent need for a large scale land reform. Such a reform program, the president insisted in his message, must be based on an easing of the constitutional provisions regarding expropriation and payment for land. The text of the amendment proposal offered by the president stipulated that expropriated land could be paid for in bonds redeemable in several payments over twenty years, with an interest of six percent, and liable to a maximum indexation for inflation of ten percent per year. The proposal also provided for the forced leasing of unused or underutilized land. The land reform bill Goulart presented to accompany the amendment proposal, which would be formally introduced to the Chamber by the PTB, stated that the purpose of the reform was to provide rural laborers with access to land to provide all with "the material and social conditions for a dignified life."[23]

Congressional party maneuvering from this point on would revolve around the issue of the presidential proposal. A special Chamber commission on land reform was created at the end of April in order to consider Goulart's agrarian legislation. The commission was to be composed of three deputies each from the PSD, the UDN, and the PTB, and one deputy each from the Social Progressive Party (a right wing party and personal vehicle of Adhemar de Barros) and the middle of the road Christian Democratic Party.[24] Thus, despite the fact that the Milton Campos bill had been introduced into the Chamber on April 5, that is, before Goulart's proposal, the president's measures would be the focus of interest from then on.

President Goulart and the PTB were determined to have the proposed amendment and law approved in an "extraordinary" single session by a two-thirds majority vote. It was hoped that enough pressure and momentum could be built up to actually get the measures ratified. The alternative was a longer process in which, during two separate sessions separated by a year, the measure was required to secure a majority vote in both houses. The PTB and its allies among the smaller parties feared that if the second procedure were used, the proposals would never be approved. There was still another alternative lurking in the wings, that of a plebiscite, as urged earlier by Prime Minister Tancredo Neves, and retired General Henrique Teixeira Lott.[25] Visão excitedly speculated that such a plebiscite could bring on a revolution, and "decree the failure of Brazilian representative democracy, which would then be ripe to welcome a Brazilian de Gaulle."[26] But this option never got beyond the speculation stage.

To secure the necessary number of votes for Goulart's objective, the PTB knew it would have to find support from among the members of the two other parties. Yet it was entirely out of the question that the UDN, with the exception of the small bossa nova wing, could be swayed in any way. It was also clear that there was no way of assuring the success for the negotiations with the majority party, PSD, in view of the fact that the deputies from Minas Gerais also seemed unmovable. The specific provisions of the PTB proposal did not in any way improve the chances for a compromise. Any constitutional change altering provisions on expropriation were bound to be considered a menace by conservatives and even moderates. The ten percent per year ceiling on the correction of bonds for inflation at a time when the prevailing rate of inflation was already eight times that made the measure totally unpalatable. Still, as the PTB perceived the state of affairs, the PSD was the only hope for passing the desired legislation.

The government was not entirely wrong in placing its hopes on the PSD. In spite of the conservative retreat it had tactically made at the end of 1962, the PSD leadership was always ready to consider any compromise that would enhance its lines of access to official power. The <u>mineiro</u> contingent was not about to change its mind about land reform, but the <u>pessedista</u> leadership decided that it had nothing to lose by negotiating with the Goulart government. Indeed, the Special Commission on Agrarian Reform had barely been formed when Gustavo Capanema, a prominent PSD affiliated jurist, began intensive work on a possible substitute to the PTB amendment.[27] Totaling up the possible votes for a suitably modified amendment, the PSD optimistically estimated the party vote in favor of an amendment would be as follows: PSD - 90 (firm) votes and perhaps another 20; UDN - 60; PTB - 20; PDC - 10; other parties - 20. This meant a total of 220 votes, or 52 short of the necessary minimum of 272.

Speculations on the breakdown of votes on land reform was entirely premature at this point. Even while Amaral Peixoto was estimating the vote, the *mineiro* deputies produced a public declaration stating that under no circumstances would they ever agree to any kind of amendment affecting expropriation of land.[28] While the PSD leadership turned its attention again to putting its house in order, the Special Commission on Agrarian Reform presented its findings on April 14. The Christian Democratic Party had been asked to report on the draft of the amendment for the commission, and it had issued a favorable statement. The Commission as a whole, however, clearly disagreed with PDC sentiments and rejected the recommendations in a seven to four vote.

At this point, the discouraged Goulart made a perfunctory attempt to meet with the party leaders of the Chamber.[29] A meeting of this type might have served a purpose *before* the special commission had presented its report. Coming as late as it did after the commission vote defeating the presidential proposal, the meeting served only to reinforce Goulart's frustration and contributed to his decision to abandon the serious programs and objectives of the positive left. He sullenly removed himself from the congressional discussion, at least for the time being. The immediate effect of his abrupt withdrawal was that the leadership of the left on land reform fell to Brizola. He, in turn, was perceived as enough of a threat to stimulate further mobilization of the anti-reformist forces, thereby polarizing the situation even more.[30]

No one was happy with the situation. UDN deputy Saldanha Derzi articulated the suspicions of the opposition that the reformist campaign was deliberately manipulated and politicized, and not a reflection of genuine rural needs. He noted that it was strange that the pressure for land reform was coming "from the General Workers' Command, from railroad workers, from dock workers, from sergeants, from bank workers, but not from those most concerned: the farmer."[31] The conservatives feared the worst was yet to come. The PTB and its allies were defeated for the moment and not encouraged by future prospects. Those who sympathized with the reformist aims and attempted to find a way of supporting the administration were, to say the least, frustrated.

In an editorial titled "7 x 4" (referring to the breakdown of votes in the Special Commission on Agrarian Reform) the Correio da Manhã addressed the urgent need for reforms in Brazil:

> But what happens? The most urgent demands of the country are introduced by a party of [PTB] pelegos and rejected by the coroneis of the PSD, now reinforced, shamefully, by the coroneis and bachareis of the UDN. . . . This two-sided demogoguery prospers because of the lack of true national leadership. . . .[32]

A member of the bossa nova of the UDN, Deputy Edison Garcia from Mato Grosso, was more explicit in his accusations, which were aimed primarily at the president himself.

> At this time, when the possibility seems remote that the National Congress will give the country an agrarian reform based on constitutional reform, it behooves us. . . to point out the responsibility of the . . . Federal Government itself, in the person of Sr. João Goulart. . . . If it be true that the [President] truly wants to give the country a reform, that fact is belied by the composition of his cabinet, by the obligations he assumes to men committed to the present economic and political structure of the country. . . . A government. . . that feasts with those it accuses of being exploiters of the people. . . [needs] to begin by serving as a

better example.[33]

For the president and the PTB, the negative report of the special commission was but the first round in its battles with the opposition in the Chamber. The next step would be to bring the amendment proposal, along with the negative committee report to a vote in a plenary session of Congress. The PTB was well aware of the fact that at this point, given the climate that prevailed in the Chamber, the proposal would no doubt suffer a resounding defeat. Stalling for time, the PTB therefore employed obstructionist tactics to prevent an immediate discussion of the amendment.

The PSD saw in this situation an opportunity to act as mediator and conciliator, thereby ingratiating itself with the government. Following directly on the heels of the report of the special commission, and ignoring the grumbling of the *mineiro* contingent, the PSD leadership produced its own proposal for an amendment. The measure was offered in an obvious spirit of pragmatic compromise. The PSD was willing to accommodate itself to the PTB position by supporting the idea of constitutional reform of those provisions affecting expropriation, and by agreeing to the principle of payment in bonds. In return, however, it insisted on a redefinition of the specific expropriationist provisions of the amendment. Expropriations could be made only of unproductive properties that were over 500 hectares (1,235.5 acres); correction for inflation of bonds would be raised to fifty percent (from Goulart's ten percent); expropriations could be made only in areas designated as part of regional plans approved by Congress; only the federal government would have the authority to expropriate land; and, finally, the Senate would have the authority to confirm the nominations to the organization established to conduct the reform.[34]

As might be expected, an official proposal to alter constitutional provisions regarding land expropriation made by the "party of fazendeiros" (landowners) itself was greeted by reactions ranging from disbelief, to apathy, to delight. UDN Deputy Francelino Pereira (from Minas Gerais) dismissed the PSD proposal as a PTB amendment in sheep's clothing.[35] Deputy Plínio Sampaio, a Christian Democrat who worked particularly hard for an amendment, observed sardonically that the PSD was finally getting in touch with national reality--whereupon pessedista Peracchi Barcelos (from Rio Grande do Sul) took strong exception to the statement, declaring to his "noble colleague, that the PSD has always been integrated into Brazilian reality."[36] A Visão editorial exulted that:

> We are. . . faced with an almost accomplished fact: that of the approval by Congress this year, within a period of three months, of an agrarian reform. This approval would signify a victory of reform over revolution, that is, of reform understood as it should be: anti-revolution.[37]

Not everyone shared this happy view of the situation. The president remained withdrawn and silent. The PTB however, had no reservations about expressing its displeasure with the PSD proposal. It pronounced the PSD proposal a pretext for setting up a thriving real estate business, and a sell-out of the principle of land reform which, the PTB felt, should put the burden of the cost on the landowners themselves, who were responsible for social and economic exploitation in the countryside.

The first half of the second phase of the agrarian policy debate thus ended on a discordant note of disillusionment and incipient radicalization. The president's program of "responsible reforms" had not met with the enthusiasm he looked for on the part of the moderates, and had drawn the criticism of radicals growing impatient with the administration's failure to produce reforms both in policy and in practice. Goulart's reaction to the situation was to abandon the "positive left" and give himself up to the politics of populist radicalism.

Jango's renunciation of the positive reform approach did not in any sense mean that he was rid of the necessity of dealing with Congress. So long as he was operating within the rules of the game, and especially because of the narrowness of his support among established elites, the Congress would continue to be the source of any and all reformist measures he wished to see passed. Consequently, Goulart's credibility with his own labor constituency had to be based not only on a radicalization of his rhetoric and on his support for strikes and demonstrations, but also on his ability to convert some of his reformist promises into law. In this, he had to depend on, and therefore negotiate with Congress.

Frustration. The necessity of doing so was brought home with particular force not only for Goulart, but also for the PTB membership in the third week of June 1963, marking an alteration in the tenor of the congressional debate. The UDN, appalled at the radicalization of the country, and uneasy over the PSD's apparent willingness to at least entertain the idea of a constitutional amendment, decided to make doubly sure that the PTB amendment proposal would be defeated at whatever point it was brought to a vote. The UDN strategy centered on a revival of the Milton Campos bill, which, following its approval by the Senate, had been shelved by the Chamber in order to deal immediately with the Goulart-PTB measures. On June 18, despite PTB and PSD efforts to prevent a quorum by urging their members to absent themselves, there were enough deputies present to approve the UDN motion to have the Campos bill reclassified "urgent" and therefore brought up for immediate consideration.[38] As a result, despite any objections the PTB had to the PSD amendment or reservations as to a possible partnership, the labor party put them in abeyance for the time being. The time for the vote on the Campos bill was fast approaching. Concerned that the bill might stand a chance of passing unless the PSD declined to support it, Goulart called in Mário Martins Rodrigues, PSD leader in the Chamber, for a conference. The president argued strongly for the necessity to enact a land reform law accompanied by a constitutional amendment. He noted with displeasure that the PSD had helped reject an unfavorable report on the Campos bill in the Economic Commission of the Chamber and thereby had contributed to its chances of passage. Rodrigues obligingly responded that the PSD was not against a constitutional amendment, and would be most happy to cooperate with the government provided, of course, they could agree on an amendment more moderate than the Goulart-PTB draft.[39]

At this impasse, Goulart could have opted to allow the Campos bill to be considered immediately, and even passed, since he could always veto it. However, he was well aware that this would delay consideration of his own measures by several months, and could even pose the danger that Congress might override his veto. This was a risk Jango was not prepared to run. Within three day's time, Goulart and the PSD leadership in the Chamber had worked out a compromise formula, closely resembling the original PSD amendment proposal.[40]

Although the president and the PSD leadership had agreed on a formula, the success of the new partnership and its ability to defeat the Campos bill depended on the approval of both the *mineiro* wing of the PSD and of the general membership of the PTB in the Chamber. The former evidently was less of a problem than the latter. The PSD deputies granted approval to the formula within two days of the presidential agreement with the PSD. The PTB, however, was not so docile, and its radical faction was reluctant to offer even formal support regardless of the immediate advantages. The PSD, determined to preserve the terms of the bargain, made it clear that unless the PTB supported the compromise, it would not guarantee that its deputies would vote against the Campos bill.

The month of July was given over to finding a way of reconciling the competing interests and ideologies of the PTB and the PSD while avoiding a definitive vote on the Campos bill. The *Estado de São Paulo*, one of Brazil's most prestigious newspapers, expressed incomprehension over the failure by opponents of the Campos bill to act, since they could have contributed to a quorum with their presence.[41] The deputies were, of course, aware of this. But the PSD wished to avoid a vote on the bill until the PTB committed itself to supporting the *pessedista* amendment proposal. Once the votes were taken, the PTB might no longer be in nearly so conciliatory a mood. In the two week period from July 24 to August 7 the Campos bill was brought up for a vote seven times, without its backers being able to raise a quorum. To break the impasse, the PSD was forced to decide whether it would take the word of Goulart and of his supporting faction in the PTB as a sign of formal agreement on the compromise proposal, or, more realistically withhold its support until, and unless the radical ideological wing of the PTB, the *compactos*, agreed to the measure as well. Ultimately, the PSD desire to accommodate itself to the situation and get the vote over with before the *mineiros* again became unmanageable prevailed. As a result, the Campos bill was finally voted on in a quorum on August 7, 1963. The votes were 69 for, and 164 against, with two abstentions. The Campos bill was formally dead.[42]

To a group of deputies from several parties who had watched this strategic play evolve and fail, it seemed self evident that any proposals originating with the PTB or the UDN were bound to go down in defeat, not because of the intrinsic qualities of the measures, but because neither party would vote for any bill introduced by the other. Some way had to be found out of this impasse, if only to be able to go on to other congressional business. Accordingly, even before the final vote was taken on the Campos bill, a new solution was being considered to the agrarian legislative impasse. A prominent UDN politician approached Deputy Aniz Badra, a Christian Democrat from São Paulo, and pointed out that the Campos bill had passed the Senate, and would have also passed the Chamber, if it were not for the strictly political issue of sponsorship.[43] If a similar bill were to be introduced by a deputy from a "neutral" party, the chances that it would be approved in the Chamber with most parties supporting it, including a portion of the PTB, were very good.

Within eight days Badra had patched together a what appeared a modified version of the Campos bill, and obtained the necessary number of signatures to have it put on the calendar of the Chamber. As anticipated, even the Goulart faction of the PTB was persuaded to lend its support by the argument that this was the only way out of the impasse, and that the PTB amendment would still be considered, albeit separately. Also, support for scheduling the bill did not imply an obligation on the part of the PTB to vote for it later. The Badra bill was officially introduced on August 6, one day beforethe Campos bill was defeated, as anticipated.

Exhausted by the frenzied activity around the agrarian issue, the leaders of the PSD majority, Tancredo Nêves, and the UDN minority, Pedro Aleixo, proposed that the debate on the PTB-Goulart amendment be postponed for ten sessions. The suggestion was readily approved. The month of August was a dead month in terms of the agrarian issue. Even newspapers reduced their intensive coverage of agrarian unrest to a mere few articles. The PTB-PSD discussions on the compromise amendment degenerated into a parlay on appointments and agreements by which the PSD might be induced to change the constitutional provisions on land reform.[44]

These doldrums, and the desultory negotiations between the PSD and the PTB dragged to an end by the end of August, when the PTB leader in the Chamber, Bocayuva Cunha, announced on the 29th of August that it was time to resume the discussion of the amendment and stop shirking the "historic responsibility" that the deputies were facing.[45] The PTB had clearly come to a final determination as to what to do about the amendment and the discussions with the PSD. The compactos -- i.e., the ideologues -- had prevailed within the party, with the result that the Goulart-PTB compromise was rejected in preference to the original version of the amendment drafted by the PTB. If there had been any doubt before, it was clear now that the alliance with the PSD forged on the eve of the vote for the Campos bill had been very ultilitarian indeed.

The discussion of the Goulart-PTB amendment was to be the final important encounter between the sponsors of the measure and the opposition. However, little effort or interest on the part of the government actually went into this last contest in the politics of conciliation. The president remained aloof and uninvolved in what he doubtlessly considered an inevitable defeat, thus contributing to the hopelessness of the situation. Considering the importance of both the occasion and the issue, the discussion of the amendment began most inauspiciously on September 6. Out of a total of 409 deputies, only 40 were present. Of these 40, only four were members of the PTB. The labor party clearly considered the defeat of the amendment to be a foregone conclusion. As the Correio da Manhã commented, "The other one hundred five deputies of the PTB were notable only by their absence."[46]

The discussion of the next month, prior to a final vote on the Goulart amendment, consisted of a reiteration of by now familiar political positions.

After several unsuccessful attempts, a quorum was finally secured on October seventh. A total of 72 votes were needed to approve the amendment.[47] In an atmosphere of depression and disillusionment, the amendment went down in defeat, with 121 votes for, and 176 against it. As if to emphasize that this was the end of an era, the government promptly dismissed Deputy Bocayuva Cunha as PTB leader in the Chamber. For the PSD, this action constituted final proof of the absence of any serious commitment on the government's part to find a solution to the legislative impasse. The tenuous PSD -- government alliance was at an end.

Phase III: The Politics of Disintegration

The defeat of the amendment signified the end of legislative discussion of land reform. It also marked the end of political dialogue and conciliation as a government strategy to attain its reformist objectives. Signaling the onset of a new politics of confrontation, the president requested decree powers from Congress in October 1963. Recognizing the futility of the request, which recalled the crisis precipitated one year earlier by Jânio Quadros, Goulart quickly withdrew the proposal.

Congress was clearly relieved. There was no possibility that it would have acceded to such a request (the military permitting) since it would have enabled Jango to attain by other means what Congress was unwilling to grant through ordinary legislation. But discussion of decree powers would have constituted still another element of controversy in an already impossible impasse.

Congressional relief over the elimination of

this additional source of strife was mitigated, however, by Goulart's total withdrawal from any further political dialogue with Congress. This act left Congress severely reduced in influence. So long as the president dealt with the legislature, the latter could exert some influence over the course of events. His rebuff left Congress in the role of an anguished and impotent spectator. At the close of the normal session, it continued to sit in extraordinary session for the duration of the recess, while SUPRA, the agrarian reform agency, became the new focus of public attention.

Within Congress, all deliberation on pending agrarian legislation was suspended while discussion centered on the forthcoming SUPRA decree which would give the president power to expropriate land along roadways, dams, and wells. The PTB and small leftist parties absented themselves entirely from these discussions, while PSD and UND representatives monopolized the floor, calling unsuccessfully for the abolition of SUPRA.

In forsaking his congressional strategy, Goulart made the decision to abandon any semblance of constitutional and conciliatory behavior. His only alternative avenue of influence lay in mobilizing mass support for his radical policies and bringing it to bear on the conservative opposition both within Congress and the nation as a whole. In other words, Goulart's strategy shifted from accommodation and conciliation within the political system to a policy of confrontation about it. Unfortunately for Jango, he raised the stakes of the conflict without adequate power to prevail against the corporate elite. Radical demonstrations succeeded in shaking but not intimidating conservative forces. Ironically, once Goulart opened the contest to extra-constitutional means of resolving the existing impasse, he virtually set into motion predictable patterns of corporatist mobilization and repulsion. Thus, his radical populist measures succeeded not in bringing about needed structural reforms in Brazil, but in paving the way for military takeover and the return to authoritarian rule.

THE CONGRESS AND CASTELO

Congressional discussion of land reform under Castelo Branco was strikingly different from what had gone on under Goulart. For reasons examined earlier, the nature of executive-congressional relations had rather dramatically changed, giving the executive an advantage even in the treatment of an issue potentially as redistributive as land reform. The actual amount of time Congress had for the discussion of the land reform law and constitutional amendment introduced by the president was severely limited. This was only in small part due to the purge of leftist representatives. Congress had its agenda full of important issues generated by the revolution. More important, however, once the measures themselves were submitted in October 1964, the Congress had only thirty days in which to decide what it was going to do with them. Otherwise, it risked witnessing their automatic passage into law, unaltered,at the end of that period. The overall character of the legislative debate on land reform under Castelo was thus quite different since actual discussion of the proposals, even during the time they were up for consideration was much more circumscribed than previously. The legislative constraint and the censorship imposed by the new regime were reflected in the fact that newspaper coverage of land reform, which before had been intensive, was now practically non-existent. As much as it was an issue of foremost public concern before the revolution, agrarian reform seemed to be an internal matter to be settled between the president and the politicians in Congress who had contributed to the success of the revolution. To be sure, the privatized atmosphere of the discussions was in no small part due to the fact that an important sector of the political public which existed at the time of Goulart was now purged, its political rights abolished, many of its leaders exiled or in prison, and its membership placed under strict observation and control. This was true of the radical political leadership, the urban workers, and perhaps most importantly, for the fledgling rural organizations, which perished under the blow of the revolution.

Within Congress, the mood among deputies supporting the revolution was somewhat somber, but relaxed. The purge of the populist part of the political spectrum left the Congress provisionally in the hands of the UDN and a good part of the PSD. The UDN now became the government party, and basked in the knowledge that "its" president was again in office to pick up, perhaps, where the hapless Jânio Quadros had left off. The expansiveness of the atmosphere prompted suggestions by some deputies that those involved in agricultural disturbances (promoting land invasions, demonstrations, squatting), be given an amnesty.[48] The Badra bill, which had been introduced into the Chamber on an urgent note and debated off and on while the Goulart-PTB amendment was being discussed and even during the first week after the revolution, seemed to have been forgotten in the general relief of the conservatives felt over the disappearance of Goulart.

The sense of relief the conservatives were experiencing in regard to what they thought would be the demise of the agrarian issue, at least on the terms that Goulart had posed it (i.e., constitutional amendment), was to be short lived, however. By the end of May there could be no dout that Castelo was quite serious in his intention to have articles 141 and 146 of the constitution amended and a land reform law passed. In point of fact, Minister of Planning Roberto Campos was already hard at work on the matter. The revolution's allies in Congress suddenly found themselves faced with the prospect of opposing their government on the very issue that had contributed so materially to their supporting the military's ouster of Jango. From the Congress, Deputy Ivan Luz appealed to Castelo: "President! Free the Revolution at any price from the infantile illness of reformism, which was so much to the taste of the adolescents of a very recent past."[49] Such appeals apparently fell on deaf ears, since even UDN leader João Mendes seemed to be unable to influence the government. An attempt to renew interest in the Badra bill as a means forestalling government policy resulted in Chamber approval of the measure in August. This maneuver in no way influenced the president's determination to secure the passage of his own measures. The consultations the president called between the land reform task force and congressional leaders seemed to be more for the purpose of informing the leaders of the president's intentions than of actually soliciting congressional opinion. The UDN, victim of revolutionary irony, again found itself in the role of principal opposition. Notwithstanding its anxiety to see the measure defeated and also to find some means of resolving the differences with "its" government, the UDN leadership could not come up with the heralded viable alternative to the presidential measures.

The castelista proposals were presented to Congress in a joint session on October 21. The UDN was ready for the encounter with over 400 amendments which would, as Deputy Cid Carvalho said, change ninety-five percent of the proposal. The major issue now was whether and how the UDN could be made to change its position. To all appearances, the old lines of battle were redrawn. The UDN was the source of opposition to the measures, the PTB was arguing in their favor (although this was no longer its government, but rather, one to which it was supposedly opposed) and the PSD, as ever, was anxious to please the government in power and follow the path of least resistance. Deputy Último de Carvalho, a landowner from Minas Gerais, member of the PSD and the congressman with the singular distinction of having made more speeches on land reform during the period under consideration than anyone else, expressed his disillusionment and chagrin with revolutionary policy thus:

> It is an irony of fate that the sponsors are the same, the very same ones, who one year ago were responsible for the political nuptials of the ex-president with the communists by means of constitutional amendment No.1 of 1963. The legislative officers are the same; the procedure -- the same; the mained constitutional principle -- the same; the amendment, in its essence -- the same, the one

> differing from the other merely in the identity of the [presidential] signatories. He of the João Goulart amendment [is in] bitter exile; he of the Castelo Branco amendment is President of the Republic.[50]

The situation was not entirely identical, however, to the extent that the UDN was now the majority party and therefore controlled the Chamber commissions. Of equal importance was the fact that the government was determined that all accommodations be arrived at in private consultation and not by means of congressional discussion.

The deadlock in the agrarian commission was finally broken when udenista Pacheco Chaves resigned as reporter on the bill for the commission and was replaced by Brazilian Socialist Party Deputy Aurélio Vianna who favored land reform and could be trusted to produce a favorable report. But the most important undertaking was to neutralize UDN opposition by prevailing on the party leadership to do away with party discipline to allow its members to vote as they wished.[51] Following intensive last-minute sessions with the president, majority leader João Mendes agreed.

With an overwhelming vote, the government thus got its constitutional amendment and Land Statute, making possible a land reform based on expropriation payable in bonds. This provision was the government's single most important victory. On other points it made the concessions and compromises which made possible the amendment and Land Statute in the first place. An accompanying amendment which would have established a separate court system for rural justice was defeated. Compensation for land would be in bonds, but any other, man-made properties on the land, i.e., buildings, roads, wells, machinery, etc., would have to be paid for in cash. Bonds would be redeemable at a value reflecting full correction for inflation. Finally, the government was only partially successful in attempting to reverse the 1961 amendment which gave _municípios_ the right to collect land taxes. The federal government would set the tax rates, but it would have to give most of the proceeds to state and _município_ governments for redistribution.

Deputy Último de Carvalho, whose bitter musings are quoted above, vacillated between despair over the possibility that Brazil was seeing the last days of private property, and the somewhat brighter thought that, as he put it, "engagement is not marriage." Between the passage of a law and the application of it much could happen. For perhaps the first time he found himself in agreement with some PTB deputies who expressed serious doubts that the government would actually carry out a land reform.

In the final analysis, the measures passed were a compromise, but one in which the government enjoyed the greater victory. For in spite of the concessions, the amendment and statute created the mechanisms making land reform possible. From this point on it would be possible for the government to expropriate property and pay for it in bonds rather than in cash. The power of expropriation, together with an agrarian law establishing institutes of agrarian reform and development constituted the basis for a broad and potentially effective policy of rural development and social change. Ultimately, however, the opinion of the conservatives that the saving grace of the measures would be the improbability of their implementation turned out to be correct.

Notwithstanding the charges of betrayal that the hard core anti-reformists leveled against the administration, they had little to fear. The Castelo land reform law was a political aberration, inconsistent with the policy course which would be followed by succeeding administrations. It was the direct result of the president's concern with rural unrest and his personal determination to grant a symbolic concession to the restive masses on whom the revolution's economic policies would weigh most heavily. Future administrations, armed with stronger decree powers, would exhibit less delicacy in considering the sensibilities of the masses.

The land reform experience was a showcase of congressional immobilism and inefficacy. As an institution, Congress was as much contributor to as victim of the crisis which ushered in an authoritarian regime. Caught in a fundamental contradiction, elected officials courted new constituencies through populist appeals while circumventing most serious attempts to deliver on reformist promises for fear of jeopardizing their immediate interests. There remains some doubt as to the seriousness of Congress' intent to participate in a fundamental transformation of the social system implied by land reform, or its ability, for that matter, to effect such reform in the face of concerted corporatist resistance. Contented to accommodate to strategies of ideological inconsistency and political opportunism, in the final analysis, they were Goulart's unthinking allies in the destruction of populist democracy.

NOTES

1. ICOPS, p.43.

2. Schmitter, p.258, Leff, pp.149-150, no. 29. Both Schmitter and Leff point out that the legislature is not generally the focus of interest group activity.

3. Eloy Dutra, IBAD, Sigla da Corrupção (Rio de Janeiro: Civilização Brasileira, 1963), p.

4. Visão, November 9, 1962, p. 12.

5. Ibid., p. 11.

6. The IPES files, for instance, contain the notation that an expenditure of $Cr. 300,000,000 was being planned to support fifteen "approved" candidates for national deputy. IPES. Executive Committee Meeting, May 15, 1962.

7. October 7, 1960, p. 15.

9. JB, January 3, 1961, p.3.

10. Dep. Aderbal Jurema, PSD, Pernambuco, JB, March 27, 1962, p.4.

11. JB, October 3, 1961, p. 11.

12. JB, June 21, 1962, p. 1.

13. Cf., JB and CM, April 21 to April 30, 1963.

14. CM, June 4, 1964, p. 10.

15. The following incident serves as an example: UDN member Oscar Correa criticized bossa nova member José Aparecido for embracing Brizola following a speech by the latter against the government's purchase of foreign companies, instead of direct nationalization. Aparecido replied that since he could not embrace the speech, with which he agreed, he embraced its author. CM, June 1, 1963, 10.

16. It had always been the majority party since 1945, and until 1961 when udenista Jânio Quadros took office, all post World War II presidents were pessedistas.

17. JB, August 25, 1961, p. 3.

18. Ibid., 28.1.1962, p.1.

19. JB, April 4, 1962, p.3.

20. Ibid., April 5, 1962, p. 3.

21. JB, May 10, 1962, p. 3.

22. Dep. Valério Magalhães, PSD, Rondônia, Anais, XXI, 1962, 174 ses., Nov. 12.

23. Camara dos Deputados, reprint of amendment and bill, p.l.

24. CM, April 23, 1963, p.6.

25. Lott who was among the generals demanding Vargas' resignation in 1954, served as War Minister in 1955.

26. May 17, 1963, p. 11.

27. CM, April 28, 1963, p. 6.

28. Ibid., May 11, 1963, p. 6.

29. Ibid., May 15, 1963.

30. Visão, May 24, 1963, p. 11.

31. Anais, VI 1968, 40 ses. May 15, p. 742.

32. May 15, 1963, p. 6.

33. IBID., VI 1963, 40 ses. May 15, pp. 690-691.

34. Ibid., Vol. VII, 1963, 48 ses., May 24, pp. 673-674. Report of Clovis Pestana, PSD-Minas Gerais defining PSD position on agrarian reform. See also Visão, May 31, 1963, p. 11.

35. Anais, Vol. XI 1963, 110 ses. July 23, pp. 379-380.

36. Ibid., Vol. VII, 1963, 49 ses. May 27, pp. 867-868.

37. May 31, 1963, p. 11.

38. CM, June 19, 1963, p. 14.

39. Ibid., July 7, 1963, p. 13.

40. The yearly correction for inflation would be to the extent of fifty percent; property that might be subject to expropriation had to cover an area of at least 500 hectares and be located at least fifty kilometers outside of cities of a

population of 50,000 or more. Also, regardless of what the total land area might be, land of which at least fifty percent was in use could not be expropriated. Correio da Manhã, 10.7. 1963, p.8, 1-2.

41. July 12, 1963, also July 26, 1963.

42. Anais, Vol. XVII 1963, 124 ses. August 7, p.181.

43. The politician in question was either Aleixo or Rondon Pacheco, according to information secured in interviews.

44. CM, August 1, 1963, p.12.

45. Anais, XIX 1963, 142 ses., August 29, p.573.

46. September 7, 1963, p.12.

47. Anais, Vol. XXVI, 1963, ses. 198, Oct. 7, pp.225-240.

48. Ibid., Vol. II, 1964, ses. 10, March 30. Waldmar Alves, PST--Pernambuco.

49. Ibid., Vol. XI, 1964, 86 ses., June 16, p.442.

50. Ibid., XXVII 1964, 204 ses., Oct. p.155.

51. This unique behavior on the part of the UDN was the product of its special relationship with the government, encouraging it to view itself as privileged, and also of the deliberate pains the president took to respect a certain degree of congressional autonomy.

5. Political Behavior and the Land Reform Debate

The institutional perspective of the preceding chapter provided a means of assessing the impact of congressional behavior on the definition and eventual resolution of issues. The observed aggregate response of the Brazilian Congress to the land reform issue consisted predominantly of a myopic preoccupation with immediate political gain modified by secondary ideological and programmatic concerns. The political strategies pursued by parties and factions with the president fixed on securing new constituencies with which to buttress existing power bases. Consequently, the exploitation of fashionable reformist issues like land reform, while appearing politically advantageous, ultimately undermined the stability of Brazilian democracy and of the Congress itself.

This chapter compliments the foregoing discussion with a closer examination of the attitudes and legislative record of the deputies in the Chamber. An analysis of the agrarian debates provides a more detailed view of what the legislators perceived to be the true political implications of the land reform issue, what they felt were the appropriate strategies under the circumstances, and how they justified their attitudes and votes.

The ensuing examination of political attitudes

is based on a content analysis of the debates on land reform in the Chamber of Deputies from 1962 to the passage of the Land Statute in May 1964. The sample consists of the one hundred eighty-six deputies who participated in the agrarian debates at any point in this twenty-nine month period.[1]

The discussion is divided into two sections. The first explores the extent to which particular attitudes on land reform are associated with the geographic origin of deputies. In other words, an attempt is made to define a deputy's propensity to support structural reforms in terms of the level of economic development of his state of origin, and particularly of its agricultural sector. The second section examines the relevance of party identification to intensity of interest and to attitudes. Besides indicating a possible propensity of certain parties for populist issues, it explores the degree to which particular parties were influenced by short-term pragmatic considerations of access to clientelistic resources enabling them to extend their power base.

REGIONAL AND ECONOMIC INFLUENCES ON LEGISLATIVE BEHAVIOR

During the periods of its existence and active participation in the governmental process, the Brazilian Congress has served as a major arena for the expression of regional interests. This regionalism has reflected the extraordinary diversity -- economic, geographic, and social -- contained within the national borders. To a considerable degree, the extent of regional power and even of representation in the legislature have been influenced by the strength and importance of regional economies. Thus, during the

Old Republic, the constitutional establishment of a federal government of equal states was mitigated by the domination of São Paulo and Minas Gerais over other states and the control this "coffee and milk" agreement exercised over the presidency.

The unequal access of all areas of Brazil to power has also been exacerbated by a bias in the electoral process toward rural states and to rural areas within states. The "politics of the governors" may have ended officially with the revolution of 1930, but the continued survival of the coroneis and of the state political machines was clearly evident after the reestablishment of electoral politics following World War II.

Since Congress enjoyed a relatively great degree of influence in the political arena during the agrarian reform debates, the legislative discussions should provide some idea of the range of regional attitudes and intensity of interest on the part of the various states in the issue. To measure intensity two indicators were used in the analysis. One consisted of noting what percent of a particular state's delegation participated in the debate at all. The second consisted of recording repeated participation in the debates by state representatives already identified as participants in the first case. The intensity of interest was then related to the general economic and demographic characteristics of that state. This procedure permits some assessment of whether the primary reason for a high degree of interest in the land reform issue is related to specific economic conditions, to political considerations, or both.

In view of the fact that the land reform debate

was allegedly generated by acute social and economic problems in depressed rural areas, we might reasonably expect that these areas, such as the Northeast, would be most prominently represented in the debates. Such an expectation is reinforced by the rural bias of congressional representation. In fact, however, the pattern and frequency of participation appears only tangentially related to rural depression and unrest. Figure 5-1, an overview of delegate participation by state, suggests that interest in land reform was greatest in the southern and eastern states.[2] This finding is clearly reinforced by Figure 5-2, which presents a regional view of Brazil. The regional demographic data indicate that the greatest participation in the land reform debate was by deputies from those regions that are the most populous, wealthiest, most urban, and have the largest electorate (literate persons over eighteen). For example, two of the most active state delegations were those of Guanabara (97.5 percent urban) and São Paulo (62.8 percent urban). It would thus appear that a relatively high degree of urbanization, and not necessarily the predominence of agriculture, stimulated interest in land reform, at least among politicians. A review of frequency of participation by individual deputies also indicates that the most interested representatives came from the most populous states, and from those with the largest electorates. The interest in land reform of delegations from the depressed, agricultural, and impoverished Northeast is outweighed by that of the South and East, where agriculture remains an important part of the economy (e.g., coffee export production in São Paulo, livestock in Rio Grande do Sul) but is commer-

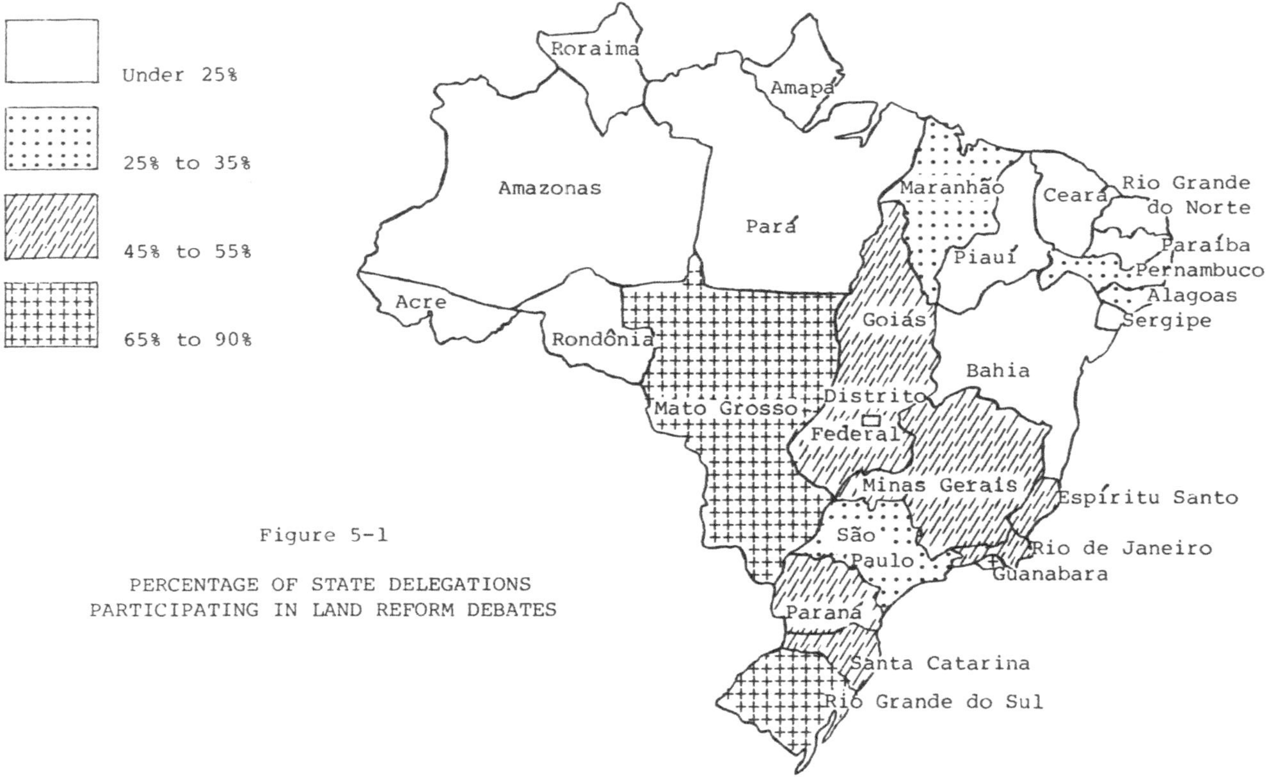

Figure 5-1

PERCENTAGE OF STATE DELEGATIONS
PARTICIPATING IN LAND REFORM DEBATES

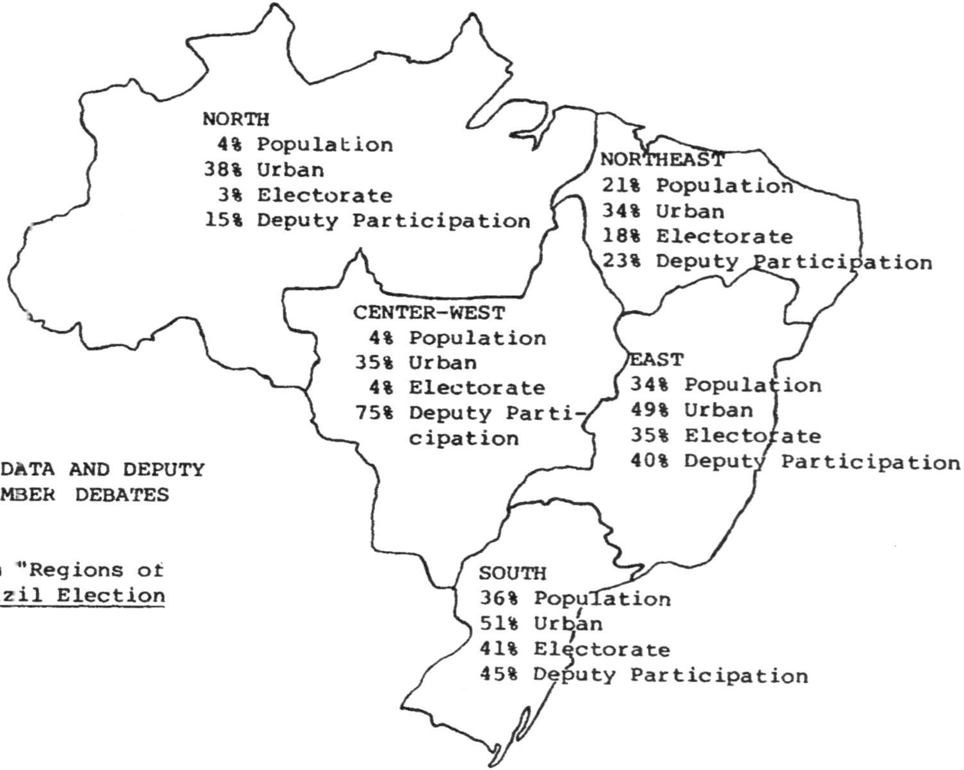

Figure 5-2

REGIONAL DEMOGRAPHIC DATA AND DEPUTY PARTICIPATION IN CHAMBER DEBATES

Source: Adapted from "Regions of Brazil" in ICOPS, Brazil Election Factbook, p.2.

cialized to some degree and complemented by relatively high industrial and urban growth. The keen interest of urban politicians in land reform might be explained by the prevalence of populist politics in their districts. Land reform, with its reformist implications, was an ideal populist issue.

In order to ascertain the accuracy of this inference, state delegations were reviewed for the intensity of their interest in the agrarian issue. Two criteria were used to indicate the states most involved in the land reform debate. One was that the state in question must have contributed at least ten percent of _all_ speeches made on land reform; the other was that at least one member of the delegation have proposed at least one measure related to agriculture. Judged by these two criteria, Pernambuco, Minas Gerais, Rio de Janeiro, Guanabara, São Paulo, and Rio Grande do Sul demonstrated greatest involvement in the agrarian debate (table 5-1). All these states were in fact at least forty percent urban at the time, although the actual percentage of urbanization ranged from a low of forty percent in Minas Gerais to ninety-seven point five percent in Guanabara. Nevertheless, a closer scrutiny of the states' economies suggests that however significant, urbanization alone does not serve as a sufficient explanation. The states in question varied considerably in degrees of urbanization. Equally significant, they differed considerably in their levels of industrialization (with São Paulo heavily in the lead), and in the nature and organization of their agricultural production. It ranged from an emphasis on commercial agriculture (São Paulo), to small independent farming (Rio Grande do Sul), to traditional

Table 5-1

STATES WITH HIGH LEVELS OF
PARTICIPATION IN AGRARIAN DEBATE

State	Percentage of all Speeches			Total Agrarian Measures Proposed
	Year			
	1962	1963	1964	
Pernambuco	11.9	(4.0)	(5.5)	2
Minas Gerais	14.3	13.1	18.2	2
Rio de Janeiro	(2.4)	10.1	3.6	2
Guanabara	(4.8)	12.1	5.5	2
São Paulo	16.7	10.0	10.9	4
Rio Grande do Sul	16.7	13.1	14.5	1
Total 6 states	66.8	62.4	58.2	13
Other 18 states	33.2	37.6	41.8	3
Total	100	100	100	16

In addition to the states included in Table 5-1, there were several other states that fulfilled one or the other of the criteria for selection into this table. Paraná contributed 10.9% of all speeches in 1964, but no member of its delegation made any agrarian related proposals or motions. Espíritu Santo and Goiás, while falling short of the 10% minimum both have records of their representatives making agrarian related proposals (cne in Espíritu Santo, and two in Goiás).

latifundia (Minas Gerais, and Pernambuco).[4] However insufficient any one demographic indicator may be for explaining intensity of involvement in the debate, the focus on an underlying political rationale appears to be well founded.

All states were, in fact, immediately and acutely concerned with the political consequences of both land reform and of the agrarian reform debate. This political interest in land reform seemed to be strongly related to a growing politicization of the population based on social mobilization, and on a trasitional phase of agricultural development.

The six states with the most active delegations experienced a high degree of social and political mobilization in the years during and immediately preceding the land reform debate. This mobilization expressed itself in political polarization and fragmentation, growth of minor, splinter parties, politicization of not only urban, but also of rural workers, and land invasions. The group consisted of precisely those states in which the social and political problems of agriculture were most pressing, and frequently the focus of national attention: e.g., the *ligas camponesas* in Pernambuco, Brizola's radical land reform in Rio Grande do Sul, São Paulo's Agrarian Revision Law, and massive land invasions in Rio de Janeiro and Minas Gerais. As a city state, Guanabara did not quite fit the picture. The reasons for its activism must therefore be located in the political and ideological consequences of the growth of radical populist politics.

The politicization of the land reform issue, and the degree to which the issue took on political as opposed to economic importance is suggested by the column of figures under the year 1963 in table 5-1. It was during this year, the heyday of political radicalism and populism, that Guanabara became intensely involved in the agrarian debate. The very highly politicized state of Rio de Janeiro found itself involved for similar reasons. The distribution of figures suggests that in these states in particular, the motivation was highly political and related to the context in which the debate developed during João Goulart's presidency.

Among these six states a small subcategory consisting of Minas Gerais, São Paulo, and Rio Grande do Sul demonstrated consistent, as opposed to non-uniform, high levels of participation in the debate for the period of analysis. Historically, the three states had a great deal in common. São Paulo and Minas Gerais, and to a lesser extent, Rio Grande do Sul, were traditionally the most powerful states in Brazil, especially during the days of the Old Republic and of the "politics of the governors." In all three states, despite great differences in levels of industrialization, commercial agriculture remained a very important sector of the economy. São Paulo is the center of Brazilian industrial development; but it is also an important coffee producer, and therefore, responsible for an important share of Brazil's export earnings. In all three states, the significance of agricultural organization lay not only in its economic contribution but also in that it served as the social basis for political control. Implicitly, for all three states, and particularly for Minas Gerais and Rio Grande do Sul, the maintenance of traditional elistist patterns of political control constituted the hidden agenda of the land reform controversy. São Paulo's slightly lowered participation in 1963 and 1964 as compared to the other two states may well be a consequence of the fact that paulista agriculture was already relatively modern, while that of the other two states was modernizing, and therefore somewhat more caught up in a transition. As Samuel Huntington observed, whereas modernity leads to stability, modernization contributes to social and political unrest.[3] It is therefore not at all surprising that the transitional states should be most concerned about the possible consequences of an agrarian reform in Brazil.

POLITICAL PARTY AFFILIATION AND ATTITUDES TOWARD LAND REFORM

Reflecting histories of eclectic constituency acquisition, Brazilian political parties evolved as pragmatic coalitions of local and state clienteles. Constructed primarily to win elections and to provide a means of distributing the patronage and favors that come with power, parties possessed little ideological coherence or programmatic unity. The larger parties in particular housed a variety of interests and constituencies. Since the major parties frequently drew on similar clienteles in building electoral coalitions, there was considerable overlap among them. For example, although the UDN stood ideologically somewhat right of center, its bossa nova section had much more in common with the moderate-left Christian Democratic Party (PDC). The difficulty in determining a party's ideological position was heightened in the case of the PSD. Its pragmatic, adaptive, and frequently opportunistic aggregative behavior frequently belied the largely conservative attitudes held by the coroneis in its rank and file.

Given the nature of Brazilian parties, the use of party affiliation as a means of establishing a member's ideological convictions can be a somewhat unreliable tool. Nevertheless, although by no means paragrons of ideological rigor, Brazilian parties could be located on a general continuum from right conservative to left reformist. Thus, parties like the Republic Party (PR) and the Liberal Party (PL) were understood to be staunch supporters of the status quo and traditional political and social values, while the Brazilian Socialist Party (PSB) and the Workers Renovation Movement (MTR) at the other end of the scale were commonly recognized as advocating fundamental social and economic reform in favor of the working class. Such a political ranking of parties in accordance with general ideological tendencies is used in this section of analysis of the congressional debates as a means of identifying the degree to which individual positions adopted on land reform corresponded to the position of the party of membership and to that party's location on the political spectrum.

The preceding chapter stressed the salience of agrarian reform as an issue with considerable political and populist significance. Observable interest in the issue appeared to be strongly related to a presidential strategy oriented toward reinforcing his power base. Reciprocally, an equally strong conviction existed on the part of opposition parties in Congress that the legislature must retain control of the issue to prevent just such an accretion of what it considered dangerous power to Jango. The manipulation of the agrarian issue for strategic political reasons should consequently be reflected in the varying intensity of the congressional debates on land reform.

Table 5-2 shows participation in the debate by party members from 1962 to 1964. In addition to indicating how many deputies from the entire party delegation debated the issue, it also records the total number of speeches made by the participating members of a party. As expected, variation in rates of speech-making on land reform parallels the demagogic manipulation of radical populist issues as a means of securing and expanding mass political support. In 1962, land reform had been singled out as a key issue by the president and was recognized as such by the Congress. Neither was inclined, however, to press for a concrete policy decision on the matter at this point. Both president and representatives made bland statements favoring land reform, but were careful to avoid sounding too enthusiastic or clear on the particulars of the issue. The radicalization of Brazilian politics and the key importance of land reform in this process were more clearly discernible in the 1963 debates. Whereas in 1962, only 42 deputies, or the total of 12.8 percent made speeches on land reform, almost three times the number, or 25.6 percent, debated the issue in 1963. Not only were there more deputies involved and more speeches made, but there was also a particularly sharp increase in the participation of members of small radical left wing parties. These parties ceased to figure prominently in the agrarian debate in 1964 as the result of the inhibiting effect the revolution had on their membership and activities. In fact, there was an overall de-

Table 5-2

DEPUTY PARTICIPATION IN AGRARIAN REFORM DEBATE, BY PARTY AND BY YEAR

Political Party	1960 Election	1962 Debate		1962 Election	1963 Debate		1964 Debate	
		Deputies	Speeches		Deputies	Speeches	Deputies	Speeches
PRP.............	3	1	1	2	1	6	1	3
PR..............	17	2	4	10	3	1	2	3
PSP.............	25	5	11	23	3	4	1	1
PL..............	3	1	1	5	3	10	1	1
UDN.............	70	6	9	97	36	71	20	43
PSD.............	115	8	10	119	15	23	14	26
PDC.............	6	6	7	19	8	15	5	7
PTB.............	66	11	14	104	29	47	14	23
PTN.............	7	-	-	11	1	1	-	-
PST.............	2	1	1	6	1	2	1	2
PSB.............	10	1	1	5	2	5	-	-
MTR*............	-	-	-	4	3	5	1	2
PTR**...........	2	-	-	3	-	-	-	-
Total.........	326	42	59	409	105	190	60	111
% of Total....		12.8			25.6		14.6	
Speeches/ Deputy......			1.4			1.8		1.8

* The MTR participated in elections for the first time in October 1962, and therefore did not participate in the debate in 1962.

** Since no deputies from the PRT participated in the debate, it is excluded from all further discussion in this study.

cline in the agrarian debates in 1964. Speechmaking fell by 11 percent from 1963. Speechmaking on agriculture remained above the 1962 level, but this might have reflected not only sustained interest in land reform but also the fact that between the 1960 and 1962 elections the Chamber grew by eighty-three additional seats as the result of a general increase in the Brazilian population.

A principal concern of this study is the determination of what the attitudes of deputies and parties were on agrarian reform itself, and the extent to which certain political parties might have adopted particular positions for strategic as opposed to ideological reasons. The following analysis discriminates between these two concerns, and arrives at an estimation of party position and ideological inclination towards potential reform of the land tenure system and, by extension, of power in Brazil. One means of discriminating among attitudes of deputies who insisted they were in favor of an agrarian reform was to identify what the concept meant to them and whether they understood it to be an economic measure to fine tune a given situation, or whether they perceived it as a measure of social reform.

Table 5-3 indicates a positive relationship between perceptions of agriculture as both an economic and social problem. The two definitions of agrarian reform are complementary primarily from the perspective of social reform which accepts economic measures as part of a general strategy. The reverse, however, is not true. Approximately one third of those contending that agriculture was an economic problem rejected the social definition of the issue and insisted on economic solutions and aimed at in-

Table 5-3

DEPUTY PERCEPTION OF AGRARIAN PROBLEM, BY PARTY

Political Party	Total	Agrarian Problem is Economic			Agrarian Problem is Social		
		Number	% of Party	% of Total	Number	% of Party	% of Total
PRP...............	1	1	100.	.9	0	0.	0.
PR...............	3	1	33.3	.9	1	33.3	1.5
PSP...............	4	4	100.	3.6	3	100.	4.6
PL...............	4	3	75.	2.7	2	50.	3.1
UDN...............	33	26	78.8	23.4	8	34.8	12.3
PSD...............	27	18	66.7	16.2	7	33.3	10.8
PDC...............	12	11	91.7	9.9	6	75.	9.2
PTB...............	40	40	100.	36.	31	93.9	47.7
PTN...............	1	1	100.	.9	1	100.	1.5
PST...............	2	2	100.	1.8	2	100.	3.1
PSB...............	2	2	100.	1.8	2	100.	3.1
MTR...............	2	2	100.	1.8	2	100.	3.1
Total..........	131	111	84.7	100.	65	63.7	100.

creasing productivity. The margin of difference between those arguing for economic or for social solutions is widest for some of the larger parties: the PSD, the UDN, the conservative Liberal Party (PL), the moderate left Christian Democratic Party (PDC), and the right populist Social Progressive Party (PSP).

As a means of checking on the sincerity of those who felt that land reform was a social necessity, general support for land reform was compared to support for the constitutional amendment which could make such a policy effective. Table 5-4 indicates a fair degree of congruity between these two criteria. The overall difference in the figures on the two categories is relatively small. Only 7.9 percent of those favoring land reform bills seemed inclined to oppose an amendment. A closer look at figures for individual parties reveals a few anomalies, such as the fact that within the UDN a greater percentage actually came out in support of an amendment than in favor of land reform. Since the assessment was based in some part on an inclination to approve the Castelo amendment, further comment on this point will await the discussion of the impact of the political milieu on the interpretation of the land reform issue.

The most significant information rendered by table 5-4 is that, given a general ranking of political parties from conservative (top) to reformist (bottom), a favorable attitude toward agrarian reform is not as reliable an indicator of ideological persuasion as is the attitude toward the amendment. The figures on the two criteria substantiate the contention that agrarian reform was for many deputies, especially for those from center and conservative parties, an exploitable political issue whose use-

Table 5-4

RELATIONSHIP OF ATTITUDES TOWARD
AN AGRARIAN LAW AND ATTITUDES TOWARD
AN AMENDMENT: DISTRIBUTION WITHIN PARTIES

Political Party	Expresses Support For			
	Agrarian Reform Bill		Payment for Land in Bonds	
	%No	%Yes	%No	%Yes
PRP................	100.0	-	100.0	-
PR.................	75.0	25.0	100.0	-
PSP................	25.0	75.0	60.0	40.0
PL.................	50.0	50.0	66.7	33.3
UDN................	76.2	23.8	76.0	25.0
PSD................	62.5	37.5	75.0	25.0
PDC................	30.0	70.0	22.2	77.8
PTB................	2.7	97.3	5.1	97.9
PTN................	-	100.0	-	100.0
PST................	-	100.0	-	100.0
PSB................	33.3	66.7	-	100.0
MTR................	33.3	66.7	-	100.0
Total............	45.0	55.0	-	48.1

Direction of axis: Upper left (conservative) to lower right (reformist).

fulness ended at the point it actually threatened the existing distribution of economic and political power.

When a coefficient of association is calculated for the two variables (support for land reform and support for the amendment), the results in table 5-5 demonstrate that there is a high degree of positive association between the two (Gamma 917). Furthermore, using Guttman's coefficient of association, it is clear that the attitude on the amendment

(Lambda a) constitutes a better measure of prediction of attitudes on land reform than vice versa.

An assessment of ideological attitudes on land reform and on the constitutional amendment may contribute to a better understanding of party behavior during the agrarian reform debate, but it does not succeed in explaining this behavior entirely or accounting for the high degree of variation in party behavior in reference to unchanging principles or ideological implications of a given policy. To explain such ideological inconstancy, additional information must be sought in the context within which the

Table 5-5

MEASURE OF ASSOCIATION BETWEEN ATTITUDES ON NEED FOR AGRARIAN REFORM AND FOR CONSTITUTIONAL AMENDMENT

Constitutional Amendment	Agrarian Reform is Necessity			
	Number		% of Total	
	No	Yes	No	Yes
Against:				
any constitutional change..................	40	3	57.1	4.4
any change affecting property................	26	0	37.1	0
For:				
when socially necessary...............	2	49	2.9	72.1
politically necessary...............	2	16	2.9	23.5
Total..................	70	68	100.0	100.0

Coefficients of Association: Gamma 91.7; Lambda a: 89.7; Lambda b: 43.7; Lambda: 63.9.

agrarian debate develops. Two elements in particular seem to exercise an appreciable influence over the willingness of deputies to maintain or abandon a political posture. One is the deputies' estimation of whether the president in power at the time is trustworthy and competent. The other is the opportunistic urge to barter principles for power by engaging in political accommodation with perceived sources of power, be they issues or people. The struggles of the political parties for an advantage in the electoral arena by capitalizing on the land reform issue is a case in point.

The importance of these two elements can be perceived by comparing the final vote on the Goulart-PTB amendment proposal, and on the Castelo amendment proposal (table 5-6). Although differing in the scope of their provisions, both amendments were identical in their purpose of altering the constitution to make possible payment for expropriated land in bonds instead of cash. In spite of this similarity, the former proposal was defeated, and the latter approved. It is true enough that the total number of votes needed for the passage of the amendment in a single session was reduced from 272 to 205. However, the totals also indicate that if the previous rules for amending the constitution had been in effect the Castelo measure might never have been approved in 1964. Even so, it is significant that some one hundred deputies, most from the UDN and PSD, switched their votes from one year to the next, while the PTB remained steadfast in its reformist inclinations. Not all who had opposed the Goulart agrarian package switched, of course. In Último de Carvalho's words, a few deputies remained "defenders of democracy." Still, the sincerity of deputies purportedly categorically against any type of constitutional change is questionable. PTB deputy Fernando Gama noted the inconsistency in the behavior of deputies

Table 5-6

VOTE ON THE CONSTITUTIONAL AMENDMENT

Political Party	1963 (Goulart)			1964 (Castelo)		
	Yes	No	Total	Yes	No	Total
PRP......................	0	5	5	0	2	2
PR.......................	0	3	3	1	2	3
PSP......................	5	5	10	14	1	15
PL.......................	0	3	3	1	0	1
UDN......................	1	72	73	51	11	62
PSD......................	5	69	74	63	12	75
PDC......................	6	10	16	12	2	14
PTB......................	87	0	87	79	1	80
PTN......................	6	3	9	2	1	3
PST......................	7	0	7	3	2	5
PSB......................	4	0	4	2	0	2
MTR......................	1	2	3	2	0	2
Subtotal.................	121	172	293	220	34	254
Recorded Abstentions...			3			1
Total..................			296			255
Official Total*........	121	176	297	232	33	265

*The count, by party, was tallied for both years from the official roll call in the Anais da Câmara and the Diário Nacional do Congresso, respectively. There are some obvious discrepancies between the final official declaration at the end of the vote, and the voting record reproduced in the official publications. The discrepancy may be explained in part by errors in recording (failure to record certain votes, or to record properly the votes of all deputies). Such an explanation perhaps is more applicable to the 1963 vote than to 1964. In the case of the latter, there is a possibility that the difference of ten votes may be accounted for by pairing.

who almost unanimously approved the constitutional amendment to put the land tax in the hands of the _município_ authorities, yet insisted, when it came to land reform and expropriation, that they could not countenance any type of constitutional reform whatsoever.[5]

Few deputies were forthright about the type of amendment they would support, and what type they would vote against. Earlier discussion of congressional politics (chapter 4) noted the reservations many deputies had about the Goulart-PTB amendment, and the possibility that more deputies might have supported the amendment if it had been more moderate. The reverse is also true. Some deputies declined to support either the Goulart or Castelo amendment because they were not radical enough. In 1963, the Workers Renovation Movement withheld support from the Goulart measure, not because it was against an amendment, but because it felt that Goulart's flagging interest and decision to withdraw from the debate jeopardized chances for serious reform.[6] In another vein, Geremias Fontes, a member of the Christain Democratic Party who was to become governor of the state of Rio de Janeiro in 1966, argued that his party should not support the 1964 Castelo amendment proposal because it gave too much of an advantage to the large landowners.[7]

Not all deputies pegged their support of a constitutional amendment to the political and personal identity of the presidential incumbent. There was also an unwavering core of opposition to changing articles 141 and 146 of the constitution which survived into the Castelo administration. Jaeder Albergara, one of the few deputies to vote against the amendment in 1964 pointed out that, ironically, the land reform issue had weighed heavily in the decision to depose Goulart. In retrospect, he wondered why they had gone to so much trouble to oust Jango when the final outcome for the agrarian sector was to be the same.[8] Último de Carvalho, who also voted against the measure, questioned what assurance there would be that the successor to the Castelo regime would live up to the seriousness of Castelo's promises and intentions? Furthermore, he asked, what if Goulart were to return by some chance, to find the right to property violated by the "hands of the democrats themselves?"[9]

Table 5-7

WILLINGNESS TO TRUST THE GOVERNMENT
WITH AGRARIAN REFORM

Political Party	Regime							
	Goulart				Castelo			
	Number		% of Party		Number		% of Party	
	No	Yes	No	Yes	No	Yes	No	Yes
UDN..........	38	5	88.4	11.6	12	9	57.1	42.9
PSD..........	17	5	77.8	22.7	6	5	54.5	45.5
PDC..........	3	7	30.0	70.0	4	4	50.0	50.0
PTB..........	1	40	2.4	97.6	1	18	5.3	97.7
Total......	59	57	50.9	49.1	23	36	39.0	61.0
Total all Parties....	73	67	52.1	47.9	26	38	40.6	59.4

The political sponsorship of the agrarian package and personal confidence in the president clearly weighed a great deal in the minds of many deputies. Table 5-7 offers some suggestion of how the members of major parties viewed the two presidents' ability to handle the agrarian reform responsibilities. The PTB consistently remained supportive of the agrarian issue, even if it were implemented by another administration. On the other hand, both the PSD and the UDN obviously had greater confidence in putting land reform in the hands of Castelo Branco than in those of João Goulart.

Assuming that support of the consitutional amendment, regardless of who proposed it, was the most accurate indication of ideological position, basic attitudes on the amendment were crosstabulated with attitudes reflecting the degree to which the political identity of the government in power influenced the final decision of the deputies on the amendment.

Table 5-8

RELATIONSHIP OF ATTITUDE TOWARD PRESIDENT AND ATTITUDE TOWARD AMENDMENT

	Government is Important			
Favors Amendment	No	Yes	Total	% Total
No....................	25	24	49	47.6
Yes....................	26	28	54	52.4
Total...............	51	52		
% Total............	54	46	103	100

Table 5-8 indicates that only 25 percent of the deputies in the sample were categorically against the amendment regardless of which government was in power at the time. Only a slightly greater percentage would have voted for an amendment regardless of who was in power. In other words, approximately one half of all the deputies in the sample made their vote conditional on the identity, both political and personal, of the incumbent president.

The above table is based on and well illustrated by examples of discussions from the Chamber debates. For instance, Deputy Brito Velho, a member of the Liberal Party from Rio Grande do Sul, was known as a long time supporter of land reform. Yet, in the discussions of the Goulart proposal, he indicated that he would vote against the amendment (as indeed he did when the time came). When accused by other deputies of being a turncoat, he defended himself against the charge by saying he not only favored an amendment, but that he had even drafted an amendment proposal himself. At this point, PTB deputy Alceu de Carvalho accused Brito Velho of lacking confidence in the government's ability to carry out a land reform. Brito concurred: "/I have/ very strong doubts in regard to its capability."[10] Udenista Taurino Dantas echoed these sentiments when he said he was less concerned with how expropriated land would be paid for, than he was with putting land reform in the hands of an inept and politically opportunistic government.[11] Another congressman who opposed the Goulart proposals remarked to me in an interview that the Goulart-PTB proposal had its merits, but could not be entrusted to that regime which in his view consisted of a "gang of illiterate leftist demagogues."

SUPRA, the agrarian reform agency, came in for a heavy share of the blame for contributing to the Goulart administration's untrustworthy image by encouraging unrest in the countryside. Cid Furtado lamented that "administrative organs like SUPRA, which are urgently needed, are extremely suspect because of the /radical/ ideology of various persons holding directing positions."[12] Assailing the administration's knowledge of real conditions in the countryside, Geraldo de Pina alleged that João Pinheiro Neto was unqualified for the job and unfamiliar with its subject matter. "It is likely," he charged, "/that he/ has never seen a rice plantation, or heard the lowing of an ox. . . ."[13]

The trustworthiness of the president and his aides was not the only issue at stake in the decision to provide or withdraw support from certain measures. Another important consideration, although the reading of the data is not as clear on this point, was the identity of the political party authoring or sponsoring a particular measure. In order to get some indication of the relationship between attitudes on the Goulart-PTB amendment and attitudes on other measures discussed in the Chamber, attitudes on the Goulart-PTB amendment were run against attitudes on the Campos bill, the PSD-PTB compromise amendment, the Badra bill, and Castelo Branco's agrarian bill. Table 5-9 does bear out to some degree the contention that political opportunism in the guise of electoral maneuvering played a key role in political decisions in Congress. In their most essential lines the Campos, Badra, and Castelo (Land Statute) bills were quite similar, yet the reaction to them differed. The PTB and other left wing parties which were committed to land reform were less likely to allow the party sponsorship in Congress and the identity of the president to influence them <u>against</u> a particular measure than were the conservative parties. Also, judging by the success of the Badra bill, it appears that the radical character of a proposal was not

Table 5-9

ASSOCIATION BETWEEN ATTITUDE TOWARD THE GOULART-PTB AMENDMENT, AND ATTITUDES TOWARD OTHER AGRARIAN BILLS

	Approves Goulart-PTB Amendment		
Approves	No	Yes	Total
Campos Bill			
No....................	8	29	37
Yes....................	37	10	47
PSD-PTB Amendment and Bill			
No....................	60	1	61
Yes....................	10	35	45
Badra Bill			
No....................	4	16	20
Yes....................	24	10	34
Castelo Amendment and Bill			
No....................	30	2	32
Yes....................	15	49	64

necessarily a determining factor for the PTB and the left which voted for the Castelo land reform package in 1964. At this point, the passage of the measures was assured not only by an alteration in the procedure for amending the constitution, but also very substantially by the decision of members of conservative parties to change their position and vote for the amendment. The change of attitude by Congress as a unit reflect not so much a change of heart on land reform, as it did the installation of a new regime regarded as more trustworthy by conservative parties.

The change in the behavior of the deputies was not necessarily an indication of ideological betrayal. On the contrary, as Milton Rokeach has pointed out, "an attitude object is always encountered within some situation, about which we also have an organized attitude."[14] In the final analysis, "behavior is a function of the interaction between the two types of attitudes."[15]

No doubt, under any circumstances, the importance ascribed by Brazilian parties to contextual political circumstances surrounding policy issues would be considered high. If the land reform debate serves as a valid example of the manner in which substantive issues are approached and deliberated, then the importance of the political context is even greater than indicated by the figures. The distortion of an issue by immediate political influences is compounded by the nature of the communication process in political discussion. During the discussions of land reform in the Chamber, the deputies seemed to talk past each other, perhaps to unseen audiences rather than to each other. Knowledge of issues, and substantive information about rural conditions and their implication were sorely lacking. As a result, since reliable information about the "attitude object," or issue, was unavailable, the importance of the context in determining operative attitudes increased accordingly. Ultimately, the final decision was determined in great part by the degree of confidence in the stability of the political situation and the relative trustworthiness of the government. A few examples from the debate will suffice to illustrate the point.

In arguing their position on land reform, the deputies frequently cited examples from Brazil and other areas of the world to substantiate their claims. Because their knowledge of the economics and social conditions anywhere was, by and large, shallow, their exchanges were frequently reduced to diatribes which to the observer seemed comic at times. A favorite ploy of the left, which spent a good portion of its time fending off charges of dangerous radicalism and sympathy for communism, was to cite in its defense the views or remarks of such unimpeachable democrats as John F. Kennedy, Lord Hume, various Brazilian bishops, and even Nelson Rockefeller.[16] This strategy occasionally backfired, as when conservative PSD member Peixoto da Silveira lashed out against land reform and any of its supporters regardless of how impeccable their democratic credentials. The Alliance for Progress and the speeches of President Kennedy on land reform, he insisted, had the sole objective of keeping Brazil essentially agricultural, colonial, and poor.[17] On another occasion when the subject of an internal communist threat was revived, this time to warn that Brazil might follow in the footsteps of the Soviet Union, socialist deputy and scholar Guerreiro Ramos provided the Chamber with a detailed analysis assuring the deputies that according to marxist theory this was not about to happen. Brazil had yet to pass through a phase of capitalist development which required the elimination of a semi-feudal landowning pattern.[18]

In conclusion, the analysis of the debates in the Chamber of Deputies generally bears out previous observations about political party behavior during the agrarian debate. Ultimately, the strategies and the behavior of political parties reflected their perception and interpretation of the political situation and of their relationship to the government in power. This was particularly true of the PSD, although the other parties by no means escaped the tinge of this type of pragmatism and opportunism.

Ideology, however, was not totally irrelevant. Although political party attitudes and behavior did undergo some modification from one set of political circumstances to another, there existed an undercurrent of firm opinion on the agrarian issue (i.e., attitude toward object) that remained largely unmodified over the years of the debate. The best example of this was the mineiro wing of the PSD and the UDN, as well as the ideological core of the PTB.

The lasting impression of political interaction in the Brazilian Congress is that of a clientelistic marketplace where certain commodities may never come up for sale or barter, but where many others are traded off cannily by the shrewed political merchants, always on the lookout for a political bargain or a new contact. The picture also has some of the characteristics of an elaborate stage production where roles are played and lines recited in an opera buffa. In the dramatic ritual, elaborate eulogies about the personal characteristics of a certain "noble, wise, learned, esteemed, and virtuous" colleague are transformed into vehicles of personal insult and political vendetta. One has the impression that the self importance of the actors is a reflection of the absence of a stage director or of a consensus among the actors on how the play is to be concluded. In the case of land reform in Brazil, the sobering reality was reintroduced with the military coup which, while appearing initially to bear out the desires of the actors, eventually caused them to recite from a new script.

NOTES

1. See the Appendix for a reproduction of the code and methodological note.

2. Mato Grosso appears as prominent as it does because of a small but very active delegation. All demographic information is based on 1960 figures taken from the Anuário Estatístico.

3. Huntington, Ch. 5, "Revolution and the Political Order, pp. 264-343.

4. By emphasizing one type of agricultural activity in a certain state, we do not mean to imply that others do not exist. Minas Gerais also has commercial agriculture and São Paulo, latifundia.

5. Fernando Gama, PTB, Paraná, Anais, Vol. VII, 1963, 49 ses., May 27, 824.

6. Derville Alegretti, MTR-São Paulo, Anais, Vol. XI, 158 ses., Sept. 10, pp. 599-604.

7. Anais, Vol. XXVIII 1964, 206 ses., Oct. 26, p. 492.

8. Albergara, PSD, Minas Gerais, Anais, Vol. XXX 1964, 218 ses., Nov. 9, pp. 560-61.

9. Anais, Vol. XXVIII 1964, 202 ses., Oct. 21, p. 692.

10. Anais. Vol. VII, 1963, 47 ses., May 22, p. 607.

11. Anais, Vol. XII, 1963, 89 ses., July 2, p. 707.

12. Anais, Vol. VI, 1963, 38 ses., May 13, p. 419.

13. Anais, Vol. I, 1963/1964, 7 ses., Jan. 17, p. 358.

14. Milton Rokeach, Belief, Attitudes, and Values (San Francisco: Jossey-Bass, Inc., 1969), p. 119.

15. Ibid., pp. 127-8.

16. See, for example, Chagas Rodrigues, Anais, Vol. VI, 1963, 37 ses., May 10, pp. 251-56.

17. Anais, Vol. XXIX 1963, 178 ses., Sept. 24, pp. 199-203.

18. Anais, Vol. XI, 1963, 157 ses., Sept. 10, p. 555.

6. The Policy Process and Conservative Modernization

Success in policy making rests in a mastery of the rules of the game, or alternatively, the ability to redefine them. In either case, skillful pursuit of policy objectives requires a sensitive appreciation of both the possibilities for change and the limitations on reform imposed by existing institutions and interests.[1] Jango's failure to achieve his agrarian program was directly related to his misperception and even disregard of the limitations on his policy choices within the existing framework. On the other hand, Castelo's ability to secure a land reform law must be understood not only as the result of wiser political craft and more propitious circumstances, but also of prudent observance of the policy constraints imposed by influential conservative elites.

In the case of Brazil, as in most Latin American countries, the viability of a sweeping redistributive policy would have required one of two preconditions. First, either through revolution or gradual attrition, the power of established elites would have had to be significantly weakened and that of new reformist and mass based leadership proportionately enhanced. Alternatively, such a policy would have required decisive support from a left-wing, reformist military acting in opposition to established social and economic interests. Unlike Cuba, an example of the first case, or Peru, an example of the second, Brazil had neither a revolution, nor a nationalist reformist military in control of the country. Behind the populist reformist façade of the Goulart administration, conservative interests retained their control of traditional political institutions and the support of the armed forces. Furthermore, despite the sympathy of some military officers for Basic Reforms, the revolutionary features of Jango's policy goals were perceived by the majority of the military leadership as a threat to some of their primary objectives. Most importantly, in their view, an emphasis on redistributive social justice and high rates of social mobilization would hinder the emergence of Brazil as a major world power and impair national security by inviting Communist infiltration. As demonstrated by the record of the post 1964 administrations, the armed forces decided that both objectives required the consolidation of a sophisticated military and industrial capability founded on a program of capital intensive development, diversification, and systematic national integration and centralization. While not precluding reforms, this program required that any new agrarian policy be subordinate to the general political and economic goals of a modernizing conservative leadership.

STRATEGY AND STYLE IN POLICY MAKING

With respect to land reform, there were clear limitations on the type of program that Brazil's corporatist establishment was willing to tolerate, and Jango's proposals fell beyond the limits of its toleration. But to ascribe his failure to achieve an agrarian reform program to a monolithic reactionary opposition is too simplistic an explanation. It assumes on the part of the latifundistas an unrealistic degree of power and sway over other interest sectors and attributes to the Brazilian policy process a rigid ideological character that is belied by a history of pragmatic, incremental decision making within a conservative framework.

Evidence gathered from interviews and published sources suggests that industrial and commerical elites had little understanding or sympathy for the problems of their counterparts in the agrarian sector.[2] However, they quickly discovered compelling reasons to be concerned for the landowners' problems when Goulart used land reform as a political threat not merely against traditional latifundia owners, but also against all established economic interests. Furthermore, once denied routine access to the presidency and to opportunities for negotiating over policies affecting their perceived domain, these interests were unified. Bound by their perception of a common threat, they resorted, in effect, to a residual veto power by deposing the offending administration.

Earlier in this study, the discussion of how Brazilian interest groups impact the policy process pointed out their relatively ineffective lobby activity, lack of organization, and absence of reliable knowledge and meaningful communication within and among their associations. In an interest structure both highly fragmented and weighted in the president's favor, specific interests have had considerable difficulty preserving their concerns against executive determination to pursue particular policy goals. This was evident, for example, in the case of the supposedly powerful agricultural sector (especially the coffee growers), which acquiesced to de facto subsidy of industrialization during the Vargas dictatorship. Even within "democratic" periods, which encouraged decentralization and regionalism and permitted greater exercise of interest group pressure, the Brazilian president could wield considerable power over policy through the use of clientelistic benefits, patronage, and the manipulation of dependent corporatist organizations. Corporatism and clientelism, by preserving personalistic, dyadic loyalty and interest fragmentation, enhanced executive power at the expense of developing effective interest articulation by grass roots organization. However, elite interests collectively retained a decisive control over the framework within which the policy process took place. The power of the state, as expressed through the executive, lay in its legitimacy as a mediator of interest and an arbiter of conflicts within an established elite biased framework. Jango undermined his own legitimacy not because he challenged a particular interest, but because he in effect attacked its source, the fundamental political framework itself.

From this perspective, Leff's provocative interpretation of executive discretion and decision making power may be viewed as both insightful and deficient.[3] His observations on four cases of economic policy making pertain primarily to circumstances in which the president successfully and safely played by the rules of the game. His conclusions provide little basis for understanding the process of a policy issue like land reform, which, contrary to established practice could not be contained by the deliberations of executive bureaucrats, but instead overflowed into a passionate and widespread public debate abetted by presidential design. In E. E. Schattschneider's terminology, Jango, like Vargas before him, was trying to prevail with his policies by "socializing" the conflict over the issue.[4] He was, in other words, attempting to redefine the balance of power in the political system by expanding the field of participants and tipping the balance in his favor. But Getúlio's shrewd cultivation of the urban working class was an adjunct of a development plan that reinforced the corporatist political framework and served the interests of the growing industrial sector. Moreover, it enjoyed the support of the military and even, reluctantly, of the middle class liberals. In contrast, Jango's strategy for welding a new reformist political coalition gained few friends and made powerful enemies. From the beginning, his strategy fatally overestimated the strength and constancy of his populist allies and underestimated the resourcefulness and determination of his corporatist opposition, its ability to respond decisively to a threat, and to secure the sympathy of the armed forces.

Jango's performance in the executive office evinced profound frustration over the contradictory pressures created by imposing a populist representative democracy on a corporatist authoritarian framework. Possessed of neither the propitious circumstances nor the political astuteness of Juscelino Kubitschek, Jango found the simplicity of sweeping revolutionary reforms an irresistable course of action. As Hirschman observed in his discussion of land reform in Colombia, "revolution requires 'only' the violent overthrow of certain ruling groups. . . whereas reform requires a special combination of circumstances, a sequence of moves in the course of which the ruling groups acquiesce to, or even connive in, the nibbling away of their own privileges."[5] Jango aggravated rather than lessened his policy problems by insisting that the ruling groups acquiesce not merely to the "nibbling away of their own privileges," but to allowing the lower class to gobble up the whole pie.

To some extent, then, Jango's failure to achieve his policy goals seems the product of a self fulfilling prophecy. His comprehensive reform approach reflected two important errors of judgment. It denied the possibility that reforms could be introduced incrementally and overestimated the political strength of the manipulated lower class as a counterweight to the power of conservative interests and established institutions. By approaching agrarian policy as if Brazilian society consisted of a small exploitative and backward landed elite on the one hand and a mass of landless workers on the other, Jango imputed to the decision making structure an unrealistic degree of monolithic inflexibility and an inability to accommodate reform of any kind. Under such circumstances, the land reform debate was cast as a revolutionary struggle, short of which no progress or alteration of the rural status quo could be achieved.

Yet, in fact, Brazilian society was complex and varied, and the corporatist establishment far from monolithic or unified until the issue became ideologically defined as an uncompromising struggle between the masses and the exploiters. The <u>coroneis</u> of the

PSD, the party most representative of traditional landed interests, were willing to negotiate with Jango over an agrarian policy package that would, in fact, have been more reformist than that finally secured by Castelo. But Jango was ultimately unwilling to compromise or connive to make the landowners participants in their own transformation. He firmly supported the PTB position, which dichotomized society into two oppositing parties and consequently polarized political leadership into those for and against Goulart. In this highly politicized and ideologically inflamed situation negotiation and compromise were effectively precluded.

In contrast, Humberto Castelo Branco enjoyed two distinct and important advantages in his effort to achieve a land reform law based on a constitutional amendment. One was that changes in institutional relations and in the political climate had increased the power of the presidency. The powers of the executive were not yet as sweeping as they would be after the fifth institutional act of 1968, which trimmed the Congress of its remaining powers and eliminated for the military government the bothersome vestiges of the democratic era. But Castelo clearly enjoyed greater leverage with Congress than had Jango. He also enjoyed the confidence of conservative interests and at that point was generally supported in his efforts by the armed forces. The new political climate, achieved at the cost of a massive purge of left wing leaders and organizations and the suspension of basic human liberties, did not assure, however, a complete agreement among the victors. It did indicate an assumption that there existed an agreement on general goals and that negotiation was possible over particulars. Accordingly, Castelo's second important advantage in the policy process was that his more conservative political objectives in agrarian reform assured greater support for his legislative measures, including the constitutional amendment. His circumspect proposals, therefore, provided a more realistic basis on which to negotiate with landowning interests.

Although important, these two advantages do not alone account for the successful passage of the law. Castelo's personal commitment to land reform played an important role in securing an early passage of the law and approval of the amendment. A special significance can be ascribed to his being a Northeasterner, the first Brazilian president from the Northeast since Epitácio Pessôa (1919-1922) and the second in Brazil's history. Equally important, Castelo expressed this commitment in a carefully articulated strategy. As described earlier, Castelo, his staff, and several cabinet ministers bargained, courted, explained, cajolled, and threatened. In the process, they were forced to concede several points. They emerged with a law that could not, as had been hoped, rely on the establishment of a separate system of rural justice to resolve agrarian conflicts and speed up the reform effort. They also had to accept a greater emphasis on colonization by agreeing to the establishment not only of IBRA, the Brazilian Institute of Agrarian Reform, but also of INDA, the National Institute of Agrarian Development.[6] Finally, they were left with a law which was riddled with contradictions and complexities and would possess little effectiveness without a strong presidential commitment behind it.

Nevertheless, they did achieve a law and the alteration of the constitution with the cooperation of a Congress dominated not by pro-reform interests (those had been purged and their political rights suspended), but by the retrograde interests of the UDN and the PSD. The new law did not signal the onset of an agrarian revolution in Brazil. But perhaps the point of this experience is that the Brazilian corporatist elites would not bow to a revolution or an overhaul of the land tenure system and were strong enough to prevent it. Any subsequent reform would therefore have to occur in an incremental fashion, if at all. Since 1964, land reform, as opposed to capitalist agrarian development, has been minimal. The problems in pursuing land reform occasioned by the weak law have been reinforced by administrations disinterested or hostile to egalitarian social objectives. But the existence of the law, the significance of the constitutional alteration of the terms governing the use of property, and the experiences in economic and social development attributable to the law's existence will constitute important stepping stones to a second agrarian phase which Brazil will, unavoidably,confront at some point in the future.

THE LAND STATUTE OF 1964

The despair of hard core conservatives who witnessed the passage of the constitutional amendment and land reform law was paralleled by the hope of reformists that these measures, although passed by an apparently conservative military regime, would bear the potential for beginning a land reform program in Brazil. Unquestionably, these contrary sentiments were premised largely on the fact that the alteration of the constitution made possible the expropriation and redistribution of property without tying that procedure to the availability of large reserves of ready cash. These sentiments also seemed to be based on an appreciation of the reformist determination of President Humberto Castelo Branco himself, who had exercised considerable personal pressure to secure the amendment's approval in the Congress and who, during his brief administration (1964-1967), accorded land reform a high priority. He appointed Paulo Assiz Ribeiro, principal author of the new law, to be the first director of the new Brazilian Institute of Agrarian Reform, IBRA, and gave him the rank of a cabinet minister. Moreover, IBRA was accorded the status of superministry, enjoying a priority among cabinet departments.[6] In 1965, reflecting this priority status, IBRA energetically proceeded to carry out the first comprehensive cadastral survey of Brazil's immense territory and to clear land titles. The completeness and reliability of the outcome were questionable since they depended on the declarations of the landowners themselves and many large landowners declined to cooperate.[7] But the measures were nevertheless an important first step in providing more reliable information on the land tenure system without which a knowledgeable reform effort could not proceed.[8]

Yet, most of the hopes and fears inspired by the possibility of a sweeping reform of the land tenure system were largely unfounded. According to Ribeiro, although the constitutional amendment would facilitate expropriation, massive redistribution of property was not the purpose of the new legislation. "It is not the large *fazenda* we have fought," he emphasized; "it is the large unused property."[9] The Castelo administration envisioned the law as a combination of economic and social measures which would transform Brazilian agriculture into a modern and productive sector of the economy and, in the process, eliminate the acute and politically disruptive problems characteristic of traditional and transitional rural areas. Large productive properties and agro-industrial or commercial agricultural enterprises were to be preserved and aided in their expansion and development. Social tensions and conflicts resulting from the unavailability of farm land in problem areas would be alleviated through colonization programs under the direction of INDA and, where necessary, by the expropriation and redistribution of unused or underutilized property and of minifundia. Ostensibly, then, the law would encourage capitalist development in the countryside both by eliminating the latifundium and by transforming landless workers and minifundia owners into middle class farmers. In this respect the Land Statute bore a remarkable resemblance to the goals of the *sesmarias* enacted six centuries earlier by the Portuguese crown and applied to colonial Brazil in its early developmental period.

In addition to establishing socially and politically conservative goals, the law itself constituted a weak instrument of economic reform. The cumbersome,lengthy statute (128 articles) met with little praise from those looking for either technical elegance and precision or for an effective instrument with which to alter patterns of land use.[10] As Doreen Warriner has pointed out, for maximum effectiveness, an agrarian reform law must be clear in its objectives, precise in the description of the procedures to be followed, and eschew vagueness, contradictions and complexity. The Land Statute, in contrast, was complex, confusing, and vague. Having no general application, it "required a number of administrative decisions before it could be implemented."[11] Rather than setting forth simple criteria by which land reform might be pursued, the law dedicated forty-two articles to explaining the mathematical equations by which the status and tax value of a property would be determined.[12] In its general vagueness and confusion, the new law conformed, in fact, to the Brazilian legal tradition which, Schmitter observed, served to "avoid a definitive point of closure," and allowed maximum room for reinterpretation in response to new political circumstances.[13] Or, as one Brazilian indicated in an interview apropos of the law, "Brazil has many laws, but it does not have one that says all the others have to be enforced."

Despite the hard battle for a constitutional amendment, the possibilities of expropriation were so limited as to be almost irrelevant. Although land itself could be paid for in bonds redeemable over a period of ten to twenty years (under Goulart the minimum was twenty years), all other property on the land, i.e., buildings, roads, dams, etc., required immediate payment in cash, even if they had been constructed by the government. In addition, the price of the land and all that was on it, regardless of its agricultural value, or increased value because of secondary construction, would be determined by the market and would, of course, be fully indexed for inflation. Under these circumstances, expropriation remained a costly and difficult procedure and its implementation, it follows, would naturally be limited.

In addition to the inhibiting costs of expropriation, there were procedural obstacles to a general redistribution of property. Even highly unproductive properties were protected from expropriation if they served as the site of a "rural industry." The existence of a commercial enterprise, be it agricultural, stock raising, or agro-industrial in nature on a latifundium, even if it occupied a mere fraction of the land leaving the rest idle, was enough to prevent expropriation of the unused portion. Also, property which had been legally declared a latifundium could only be expropriated if it were located in an officially designated "priority area" where demand for land and conflict were high.[14]

The difficulties of expropriating unused land did not end here. When IBRA decided which land in preestablished "priority areas" should be expropriated, neither expropriation nor assumption of titles by new owners was automatic. The owner retained the right to challenge IBRA's decision in court. Until the cumbersome Brazilian judicial system finally ruled on the matter, the land remained in the owner's control and several years might elapse before the appeals procedure ran its course to an uncertain conclusion. Only then, assuming a favorable ruling on the expropriation, could the land be distributed as family farms to the camponeses. They then became obligated to pay for the property over a twenty year period, during which time they could not resell the land.

It is not surprising, therefore, that the law

defined expropriation as a measure of last (and evidently uncertain) resort and designated progressive taxation as the major instrument of reform. With the exception of those properties located in priority areas which were declared expropriable, ununused, or underutilized, land was subject to a special land tax, the Impôsto Territorial Rural (ITR).[15] Its amount depended on the extent and value of the unused land, based on the declaration of the owner, and would increase yearly for five years up to a maximum rate of 2.7 percent. At that point, the property might be, but did not have to be expropriated. No stipulation existed that property assessments had to be indexed for inflation, as in the case of agrarian bonds. Since, for tax purposes, land in Brazil was notoriously undervalued and since inflation after the revolution remained over twenty percent a year, the tax on idle property appeared to large landowners to be more an annoyance than a believable threat.[16]

In addition to the above, the possible effectiveness of the land tax, ostensibly formulated to serve as the source of revenues to finance the agrarian program, was further undermined by constitutional restrictions on its use. Earlier, during the Goulart administration, the constitutional amendment of 1961 had transferred authority over land taxes from the federal government to the local municípios. The passage of Amendment 18 of December 1965 succeeded only partially in restoring federal authority over land taxation. The new amendment allowed the federal government to establish criteria for taxing property, but assigned collection authority to the states. These, in turn, were allowed to retain twenty percent of the proceeds, with the remainder returning to the municípios. Lest this be perceived as a means of developing local level agrarian reform efforts in the possible absence of an effective federal initiative, the Land Statute specifically prohibited independent agrarian reform activity by state governments.

Nor were the problems of the land tax entirely attributable to the exact provisions of the taxing procedure or chronic inflation. Hirschman has observed that taxing idle or underutilized property is one of the most ineffective ways to promote reform and is best relegated to the category of "gadgetry." At a minimum, the tax scheme requires realistic land values based on a competent survey, and "is usually found acceptable only when there is an imperious need for new expenditures.[17] It is also a weak political tool since "while it arouses the opposition of the landed interests [and of small farmers as well], it does not hold out an obvious appeal to any other important social group." In addition, the intended beneficiaries of this policy, minifundia owners and landless peasants, fail to perceive any direct relationship between tax measures and the possibility that landowners may become more willing to sell or rent land, or to lower their prices.[18]

The ambiguity and weakness of the law and the circumspection with which it taxed landowners or expropriated idle property indicated that Brazil had not yet acquired a reformist instrument which could exploit the full potential of the amendment for improving the lot of the camponeses. It was also clear that in the absence of a forceful and independent land reform authority, the law's application and effectiveness would depend greatly on the support it received from the president. Yet, at this point in

Brazil's history, there was little expectation that the military presidents who were to succeed Castelo would share his social conscience or his conviction that land reform was one of Brazil's highest priorities. It is therefore not surprising that agrarian policy, particularly after 1967, has conformed closely to the priorities of conservative, state capitalist development and to the implicit limitations established by the corporatist elites' veto power over the scope and direction of reform.

AGRARIAN POLICY, 1965-1975

For Castelo, agrarian reform was a matter of deep personal commitment and he accorded it a high priority in his government. But the president's priorities outside the realm of economic stablization centered not on social reform itself, but rather, on the establishment of a new, stable, political process that would support economic development and technological change with seriousness and careful management. Behind a semiliberal façade, Castelo's authoritarian technocracy set about cleaning up corruption, subversion, and inefficiency. His dreams of limited democracy and popular support were dashed, however, by the gubernatorial elections of October 3, 1965. Instead of demonstrating, as desired, a widespread endorsement for the political and economic reforms of the past year and a half, the returns showed that the PSD led opposition, encouraged by former president Juscelino Kubitschek, continued to make a strong showing.

The electoral results triggered an internal coup by the *linha dura* (hard line military) who forced

Castelo to decree two more institutional acts, the first of which, Institutional Act No. 2 of October 27, 1965, gave the government sweeping powers to suspend political rights and try civilians in military courts. Institutional Act No. 3 of February 5, 1966 provided for indirect election of governors, and the appointment (as opposed to election, previously) of mayors. A complementary act abolished the existing party system and replaced it with an official two party system in which ARENA, the National Renovating Alliance, was established as the government party, and the MDB, the Brazilian Democratic Movement, the official opposition.

In the midst of the political crisis, sharpened by already visible conflicts within the military as to its future role in the government and on the policy objectives to be pursued, social reform objectives faded from prominence. The hope for a serious attempt to apply the Land Statute, already overshadowed by the internal coup of the linha dura and the succession struggle from which Minister of Defense Arthur Costa e Silva would emerge victorious, was to disappear with Castelo's departure from office.

Costa e Silva, from whom Brazil vainly awaited a "humanization of politics," proved to be more rigid and conservative than Castelo and less adept as a leader. His laissez faire attitude toward what he could not control or understand permitted factional politics to reenter through the back door of his regime. Social alienation increased and the deepening unrest and conflict with dissident social and political groups ultimately led to another internal coup. The result was an even more repressive military rule, known as well, if not better, the world over for suppression of human rights and torture as for its economic achievements.

The watershed crisis of December 1968 arose when carioca federal deputy, Marcio Moreira Alves, publicly attacked the regime's terrorist tactics and its disregard for civil liberties. Congress' refusal to censure and strip him of political immunity provided the government with a pretext to proclaim Institutional Act No. 5 and close the national legislature. The linha dura was again able to force the hand of the president, much as it had done in 1967. The fifth institutional act extended even further the arbitrary powers of the executive. It renewed emphasis on cleaning up graft and corruption; on efficiency, purity, and morality; on centralization, administrative alignment of local with state and federal levels of government, and bureaucratic reform.

The stage was thus set for the next ten years of military government during which the armed forces could put into execution their vision of Brazil's economic and international future unrestrained by domestic bickering and subversive dissent. Within this context land reform was demoted from its priority status to take its place as a subordinate aspect of a comprehensive national strategy focusing on capitalist transformation and geographic and sectoral integration. Since 1968, the evolution of agrarian policy can be separated into three major aspects. These have consisted of the strengthening of the land reform law, the weakening of the administrative appartus that had been established to implement the law, and a close integration of agrarian policy with broader national development goals.

Reinforcement of the Land Statute

The determination of the military governments to bend all recalcitrant groups, including erstwhile allies, to the logic of Brazil's new economic order resulted in an anomalous strengthening of the provisions of the Land Statute. Armed with increased decree powers, President Costa e Silva was not required to appeal for congressional approval to revise the law. Instead, he issued a large number of decrees aimed at eliminating inefficient businesses and economically unproductive practices. Among these measures, Institutional Act Number Nine of April 25, 1969 increased the legal authority behind the Land Statute.[19]

First, it provided that the cost of expropriated land would no longer be determined by the market value of the property, but by the declared tax value of the land. Landowners were given exactly one hundred eighty days to submit final assessments on their properties. Land taxes in Brazil were by and large nonexistent before the revolution and, even after 1964, the declared value of the land for tax purposes was frequently a fraction of its real worth. The decree therefore aimed to catch the large landowners one way or another. If they declared the full value of their land, the government's tax revenues would increase; if they did not, their land, in theory, could be expropriated. Then they would receive no more than the undervalued sum that appeared on their tax declarations. To insure compliance with the registration of all properties at their actual worth, the decree required that landowners present a valuation certificate from the land tax office upon paying their income tax (another innovation of the revolutionary government) as well as upon transacting any legal and financial business concerning their property.

A second provision of the decree stipulated that agrarian bonds would in the future be subject to a maturation period of twenty years minimum and that payment for expropriated property no longer had to be made prior to the act of expropriation. This meant that the state could take possession of the land whether or not the owner agreed to the value of the compensation. Disputes over the reimbursable value of the land were to be reduced by fixing payment to the value declared for tax purposes. The expropriation process was further streamlined by removing it from the jurisdiction of the civil courts, and transferring authority over appeals and complaints to administrative offices.

These measures were a clear indication of the government's impatience with the cumbersome machinery established by the Land Statute to deal with and resolve conflictual rural problems. But if the ninth institutional act was meant to increase the central government's administrative authority, it should not be interpreted as a sign of renewed reformist fervor by the military regime. Indeed the organization reforms which accompanied the reinforcement of the land law effectively redefined the emphasis of agrarian policy by officially downgrading the agrarian reform institute and minimizing still further the role of land distribution in the overall agrarian policy.

Administrative Demotion of Land Reform

The administrative prominence of the land reform effort had begun to suffer a decline even during the

Castelo Branco administration. Following the second inner coup of the linha dura at the end of 1965, the priority of land reform gave way to more pressing political and economic concerns. As a consequence of an organizational reform in 1967, IBRA's director no longer held cabinet rank and, like the director of the agrarian development institute, INDA, now reported to the minister of agriculture instead of directly to the president.

The ninth institutional act of 1969 further blurred the distinction between the two organizations and increased their distance from the president. A number of functions that had previously been within the jurisdiction of INDA, such as colonization, were shifted to IBRA and both agencies were placed under a new administrative body, the Executive Group for Agrarian Reform, GERA, which was responsible to the minister of agriculture.

In addition to undermining its effectiveness and reducing its authority, IBRA's reorganization and frequent personnel changes also produced a negative impact internally causing a decline in morale and, eventually, the departure of some of its most dedicated staff to private industry. Originally they had to come to work at IBRA at lower salaries than those offered by the private sector because of their sense of commitment and hope that serious reform might indeed be implemented in Brazil. By 1969, in spite of the strengthening of the land reform law by the institutional act, there did not seem much point in staying on. One of these disillusioned staffers commented to me that IBRA had become "an atomic machine to make popcorn." There was no administrative authority and no political commitment from the nation's leadership to support the exercise of the increased powers and streamlined procedures of the new decree law.

By the third quarter of 1969 IBRA was no longer recognizable. The transfer of functions to it from INDA (essentially the result of personal rivalry between the minister of agriculture and the head of INDA) had reduced the agrarian reform institute to a functional copy of the Ministry of Agriculture. It was now required to deal not only with colonization, but also with extension programs, credit problems, and cooperatives. "The only thing that IBRA does not do," an irate and frustrated IBRA official fumed in an interview, "is distribute land." Debilitating politics seemed to have crept even into the one area where IBRA supposedly had jurisdiction: that of designating priority areas for land reform. IBRA's recommendations could be, and were regularly overruled by GERA. There were allegations that designation of priority areas was now motivated less by the existence of pressing rural problems than by the desire to use land reform as a gravy train for the allocation of public works and colonization projects.

The final step in the administrative demotion of land reform, represented graphically by table 6-1, occurred shortly thereafter. In October 1969, in a key speech on agrarian policy delivered in Rio Grande do Sul, Minister of the Interior Costa Cavalcanti stated that he firmly supported the existing agrarian structure and approved only of colonization as an acceptable strategy for dealing with the demand for land. The abolition of IBRA, INDA, and GERA by President Emilio Garrastazú Médici in mid 1970 and their replacement by a new autarchy, the National Institute

Table 6-1

STRUCTURE OF AUTHORITY OVER LAND REFORM

Year	Structure
1965	President ↓ IBRA
1967	President ↓ Minister of Agriculture ↓ IBRA
1969	President ↓ Minister of Agriculture ↓ GERA ↓ IBRA
1970	President ↓ Minister of Agriculture ↓ INCRA

for Colonization and Land Reform, INCRA, came as no surprise to disillusioned land reform advocates.[20]

Economic Development and National Integration

The post 1964 governments fixed their developmental goals on the attainment of sustained economic growth within a capitalist framework. This required, they decided, not just a reduction of the galloping inflation inherited from Goulart, but a reassessment of the import substitution experience of the fifties and early sixties. That experience, the economic architects of the post 1964 period claimed, resulted in imbalanced growth and distortions in the allocation of resources as a consequence of inflation and price controls.[21] Through a series of developmental plans, including the Government's Economic Action Program, PAEG (1965), the Strategic Development Program, PED (1968/70), and the Economic and Social Development Plan, PND (1972/74), they proposed that Brazil achieve balanced growth in which the "expansion of markets depends on and adjusts itself to improvement in productivity." The point was to avoid the strategy favored by CEPAL, through which a redistribution of income would "create markets without creating productivity and without concern for the future savings rate."[22] Besides bringing down inflation, these plans focussed on strengthening capital markets, instituting new credit mechanisms to increase the demand of investors, promote a redistribution of resources among regions and sectors by the use of tax incentives, and promote the growth and diversification of exports. Perhaps in part, as Baer notes, the continuation of economic stagnation until 1968 can be attributed both to the immediate effects of the stabilization program and "the time-lag involved before the effects of the institutional reforms in the financial system could be felt and the numerous studies and plans for the expansion of the country's infrastructure and heavy industries could generate actual construction activities."[23] This period was followed, however, by an extraordinary economic boom with a real annual growth rate of ten percent.

One aspect of the military governments' development plans -- the reallocation of resources -- had important implications, at least indirectly, for agriculture. Viewed as a corrollary to the agrarian program being carried out by INCRA, it actually served as a more faithful expression of recent agrarian policy than did the Land Statute. The National Integration Program (PIN), brought into existence as an aspect of the PND of 1972/74, proposed to integrate backward areas into the national mainstream through programs of regional development. "In a global sense, the purpose was to take advantage of the most abundant means of production -- land and labor -- in undertakings entailing low capital costs, that is, in ranching and farming activities and public works, without interrupting the industrialization process. This required a plan for the distribution of land, colonization, and for infrastructure [development] in transportation.[24]

The PIN established a National Integration Fund and the Program for Redistribution of Land and Stimulus to Agroindustry in the North and Northeast, PROTERRA, supported by thirty percent of the proceeds of various sectoral and regional tax incentive programs (SUDENE -- Northeast, SUDAM -- Amazon region, SUDEPE -- fishing, IBDF -- forestry, and EMBRATUR -- tourism). For the 1972/74 period, the two programs were earmarked six billion cruzeiros (eight hundred million dollars) for infrastructural development in transportation; colonization along the full length of the new thoroughfares (including the Transamazonic and Cuiabá-Santarem highways); mineral exploration, irrigation, and development of rail and river transportation corridors. PROTERRA would do for agriculture, it was planned, what the tax incentive program of SUDENE had done for industry.[25] Northeast landowners with properties classified as latifundia were faced with a carrot (tax relief) and stick (expropriation) approach as incentives to modernize their properties and make them more productive. The effort was viewed as a cooperative project between owners and workers to remedy "defective" patterns of land use and, on a voluntary basis, create small and medium rural enterprises." Clearly oriented toward the middle income category rather than the poor, the plan aimed to "eliminate the danger of merely consumer (oriented) economies, that is, of family subsistence, which do not at all represent individual progress or collective development."[26] The larger the size of an owner's total holdings, the greater the portion of the land to be involved in the program: 20 percent of 1,000 hectares; 30 percent of 1,001 to 3,000 hectares; 40 percent of 3,001 to 5,000 hectares, and 50 percent of over 5,000 hectares.[27] Under the supervision of designated financial institutions (Bank of Brazil, Credito Fundiario, ABCAR), the owner was to participate in planning the new developmental activity, contributing his knowledge of viable crops and markets, and assisting in the definition of a workable land distribution program. The watchful eye of PROTERRA and a "correct" policy of minimum prices "will prevent this relationship between the small owner and the former latifundista from being established to the detriment of the former."[28]

The Record of Reform

The meager evidence of land reform available after fifteen years of a new agrarian policy in Brazil affirms the overwhelming capitalist/developmental bias of the effort and the limited benefits yielded to the nation's poor. IBRA's initial goal had been to settle 200,000 camponeses a year on their own plots. By the end of 1966, IBRA's best period, it had succeeded in establishing only 4,000 families.[29] As of 1973, the total number of families newly established on their own property, including both expropriated and previously unoccupied land was 22,312, with over half the plots (12,408) distributed in the virgin territories of the northern states (Amazonas, Pará, Rondônia, Acre).[30]

In a review of the impact of ten years of agrarian reform policy on the Northeastern município of Caruaru in Pernambuco, a recent study noted that the problem of minifundia has grown rather than decreased and that tax, credit, and technical assistance policies have benefitted more prosperious owners. In the Northeast during the 1960/70 period, 90 percent of the increase in rural holdings occurred in the category of 10 hectares or less, with holdings of one hectare increasing most rapidly of all from 114,000 or 8 percent in 1960 to 350,000 or 16 percent in 1970. In 1960, 288,000 persons worked on these minifundia of under one hectare; in 1970, that figure had increased to 809,000 persons. Over the same ten year period, the 400,000 individuals working properties between one and two hectares in 1960 increased to over one million in 1970. In sum, approximately two million people, or a fourth of the region's agrarian work force, were working on properties of two hectares or less. Evidently, the eradication of minifundia and formation of a new rural middle class were not proceeding as rapidly as intended by the new agrarian policy and economic development plans.[31]

The existing rural middle and upper income categories, on the other hand, seemed well served by the new policies. Properties of one to two hectares were taxed at eight times the rate of those over fifty hectares, and a majority of credit applications were approved for properties over fifty hectares in size.[32] Finally, eligibility for tecynical assistance is limited to properties greater than ten hectares and, in practice, of the <u>munícipio's</u> 83 properties receiving assistance, the average size was 66.3 hectares.[33]

A major precept of those who equate economic development with capital intensive activities is that eventually traditional forms of land exploitation must give way not to a revamping of the land tenure structure, but to the consolidation of large commercial properties and the mechanization of agriculture.[34] Presumably, a policy discriminating against small proprietors should eventually maximize productivity by eliminating minifundia and encouraging urban migration of displaced individuals to find new employment opportunities in an expanding urban market.[35] In practice, however, this policy has resulted in an increase rather than a diminution of both minifundia and unemployment, especially in the Brazilian Northeast where the problem was gravest to begin with.

Moreover, this trend threatens more than just a persistance or increase in the number of rural poor. A recent study has pointed out that rather than causing "merely" or only humanitarian problems, a capital intensive agrarian development policy "has direct and important implications for increased productivity."[36] It assumes a direct relationship between the profit maximization of an individual firm and the economic well being of the nation as a whole. "There is indeed an implicit assumption that somewhere policies are being implimented to maintain full employment and that when a laborer moves from one job to another it always results in increased productivity. But these are unwarranted assumptions in cases of less developed countries. Indeed, these assumptions point to some of the critical problems of development."[37] In a situation like that of Brazil, where income distribution is highly skewed, an increased volume of commodities does not automatically create greater consumer demand or generate sufficient jobs to absorb displaced workers. Consequently, in the absence of a labor intensive agrarian policy, even the recent respectable growth in Brazilian agrarian productivity (an average of 5.6 percent in real growth terms between 1968 and 1975)[38] does not immediately benefit the rural poor, or, ultimately, serve the best interests of Brazilian national development.

THE MANAGEMENT OF CHANGE IN BRAZIL

This volume began by developing the thesis that the Brazilian political system has maintained a high degree of continuity with its patrimonial past. It has remained authoritarian and dominated within its statist framework by conservative elites. The democratic era of mobilizing populist politics between 1945 and 1964 was essentially anomalous and misleading in its illusive promises of sweeping reforms and social benefits. Indeed, the fact that an agrarian reform measure was ultimately enacted by a military regime in 1964 both affirmed the conservative pattern of Brazilian political development and served notice that incremental and conditional reformism, not populist revolution, would prevail as the dominant idiom of public policy. By the same token, intransigent latifundists who had joined the revolution to forestall any change were to find few allies among the influential industrial and commercial sectors and the developmentalists within the military regime.

The 1964 Land Statute thus capped a critical debate over the nature and pace of Brazilian development. In particular it posed the question of whether modernization of the rural sector would imply or necessitate a radical restructuring of Brazil's entire political and social order (perhaps on a Fidelista or Maoist scale); or whether it should be restricted to conservative economic measures relying on increased agricultural productivity to improve social conditions. Although the former contingency was always more hypothetical than real, the land reform issue nevertheless posed the alternatives of a mass mobilization system geared to redistributing wealth and property to the masses or of a traditional authoritarian order pursuing development within the existing corporatist, state capitalist framework.

The manner in which the 1964 crisis was resolved demonstrated that final decisions about Brazil's political future still rested with the corporatist elites and their underlying network of informal or tacit political controls. The formal "democratic" reconciliation system that functioned after World War II partially masked this reality and aggravated an important contradiction. On the one hand, the corporatist elites were the real power brokers. On the other, within the mechanisms of populist politics, they lacked direct formal means to influence policy and control its implementation. When populism threatened the security of the corporatist establishment, upper class interests resorted to extra-constitutional measures to bring about a deliberate demobilization by severely limiting public access to and participation in politics.

Viewed analytically, the apparent disruptions of political regimes in Brazil should be regarded as less a sign of chaos and lack of direction, than as an historically established mode of coping with political crises threatening an undersirable redefinition of the political system. In their use of a collective veto power over the fate of administrations and the course of development, the Brazilian political elites, with the military at the head, have reserved for themselves the right to establish the rate and means by which new contenders could be incorporated into the political system and essential conflicts over resources resolved. Such a pattern, to be sure, is not uniquely Brazilian or, for that matter, Latin American. Authoritarian rule has often been regarded as necessary in managing high rates of economic growth and social change. Planned rapid transformations might otherwise be impossible because of obstruction by specific traditional interests (such as latifundia owners) to such changes on the one hand, or the intemperate demands for immediate redistribution of wealth by mass movements on the other. Unfettered democracy under circumstances of rapid mobilization might overload the political system with simultaneous demands and lead to the destruction of corporatist influence and privilege.

Not surprisingly, to preserve their political and economic hegemony,dominant interests preferred that new social sectors enter into the Brazilian political system not as autonomous actors in a representative democracy, but, more typically, as dependent subjects of a tutorial and paternalistic order. This was true of the incorporation of the middle class in 1930 and of the urban working class a few years later in the course of the Vargas dictatorship. These additions to the membership of accepted participants in the political process reordered the relative importance of various groups within the corporatist establishment. As the focus of economic activity shifted from agriculture to industry, the corporatist leadership expanded to include new industrial and professional groups. These newcomers then began to eclipse the agrarian sector. But these changes, reflections of the pressures created by economic modernization for social and political integration, have thus far reaffirmed the continued validity and vitality of an institutional framework firmly rooted in a patrimonial past. To be sure, in safeguarding these institutions, the supporters of the Brazilian authoritarian state have not merely conformed to a preordained fate. The political and economic events of Brazilian history are also the reflection of developmental priorities and deliberate choices made by an elite determined to insure the continuity of the traditional political order and therefore of its own supremacy.

Given the improbability of a revolutionary redirection of the Brazilian developmental strategy, it would seem that a pragmatic incremental approach offers the most hope for reform. Historically, Brazil has demonstrated that it favors a style of decision making that is open ended and based on coalition building. An awareness of the flexibility of the Brazilian system must also, however, be combined with an understanding of the present leadership's priorities in order to be able to speculate about the future. On that score, it is clear that the primary objectives of the military government are the generation of wealth, economic growth, and an international status ultimately equivalent to that of the first ranking world powers. The present Brazilian leadership is in no sense willing to risk dreams of greatness (the saying goes, "God is a Brazilian") for a gamble on social reforms, the direct benefits of which may take time to materialize.

However, the military and their supporters must understand that ignoring pressures for greater economic equity and political participation by the lower classes, and particularly the rural masses, is also risky. Rural unrest in Brazil has not been abolished; it has only been contained. The social and economic conditions and political pressures that produced it in the first place have persisted and in some instances been aggravated. Ultimately, the degree of Brazil's greatness and international prominence, not to speak of the state's moral and ethical legitimacy, will depend on the creation of an institutional structure capable of absorbing changes without resorting to costly disruptions and repression. The optimal use of all its rich resources requires, in the final analysis, that Brazil devise a developmental strategy premised not on the marginalization exploitation of a large part of its population, but in harnessing the useful and willing energies of the entire nation. The ability of the Brazilian conservative leadership to make choices insuring this outcome depends to a considerable degree on their acknowledging that in the long run their security and well being are better served by incorporating the economic costs of social equity and political humanism into developmental goals than by prolonging policies of costly political repression.

NOTES

1. As Barraclough and Domike observed in an overview of Latin American land reform activity in the early sixties, choices within a given framework are possible, "but the institutional and political limits on policy alternatives are much narrower than perceived by outside observers." "Agrarian Structure in Seven Latin American Countries." p. 392.

2. In interviews, officers of industrial and commercial associations could see little, if any, relation between agrarian issues and problems and their own interests. Landowners, conversely, complained that they were routinely ignored and misunderstood both by other groups and the government.

3. Op. cit.

4. E.M. Schattschneider, The Semi-Sovereign People. A Realist's View of Democracy in America (Hillsdale, Ill.: The Dryden Press, 1960), pp. 7-8.

5. Journeys Toward Progress.

6. IBRA was established as an autarchy by Decree Law No. 55,889 of March 31, 1965. Campanhôle, Legislação Agrária, p. 194.

7. The questionnaires for the survey were distributed to landowners by the mayor of each municipio. The largest owners tended to ignore the survey both because of its potential threat to their status and also because they could dismiss the possible threat of a fine for noncompliance as unimportant. The most delinquent states were São Paulo, Rio de Janeiro, and Guanabara. Conferência, 1966, p. 17; and interviews with IBRA officials.

8. The survey disclosed, for example, that there were 1,000 more land holdings in Brazil than had been reported by the 1960 census. Also, a number of land owners discovered for the first time the actual dimensions of their property.

9. Conferência, 1966, pp. 4, 5.

10. The full text of the Land Statute, Decree Law 4,504 of November 30, 1964 is reproduced in Campanhole, Legislação Agrária.

11. Doreen Warriner, Land Reform in Principle and Practice (London: Clarendon Press, 1969) p. 292.

12. Osny Duarte Pereira, "O Estatuto de Reforma Agrária," Revista Civilização Brasileira 1, 1965, p. 25. See also IBRA, O ITR Calculado (Rio de Janeiro: IBRA, 1966).

13. Interest Politics in Brazil, p. 255.

14. Initially, priority areas were decreed in the states of Minas Gerais, Rio de Janeiro, Rio Grande do Sul, Pernambuco. These states had experienced some of the highest incidences of rural violence.

15. Much of IBRA's energy in the first months went into analyzing and explaining to others this complicated taxation system. See for example, O ITR Calculado.

16. William R. Cline, Economic Consequences of a Land Reform in Brazil (London: North Holland Publishing Company, 1970) p. 167. Cline's study is largely theoretical and reviews the law and its hypothetical rather than actual impact. Hirschman provides a more spirited discussion of alternative agrarian strategies in Journeys Toward Progress, chapter 2, "Land Use and Land Reform in Colombia," pp. 134-213.

17. Ibid., pp. 183, 184.

18. Ibid., pp. 184, 187.

19. JB, May 20, 1969 contains the text of this decree.

20. Decree Law No. 1110, July 9, 1970.

21. Werner Baer, "The Brazilian Growth and Development Experience: 1964 - 1975" in Riordan Roett, editor, Brazil in the Seventies (Washington, D. C.: American Enterprise Institute for Public Policy Research, 1976), p. 43.

22. Victor da Silva and Mircea Buescu, Dez Anos de Renovação Econômica (Rio de Janeiro: APEC, 1974), p. 39. Also see pp. 23-47 for a discussion of the objectives of the three development plans.

23. "The Brazilian Growth and Development Experience," p. 46.

24. Silva and Buescu, p. 98.

25. Ibid., pp. 98, 99.

26. Arthur Pio dos Santos, "PROTERRA, Reforma Agrária Consentida," Revista do Directo Agrário 1 (1973), p. 14.

27. Ibid., p. 13.

28. Ibid., p. 15.

29. Conferência, 1966, p. 17.

30. Instituto Nacional de Colonização e Reforma Agrária, Relatôrio Anual, 1973 (Ministerio de Agricultura, 1973), pp. 33-35.

31. Douglas Young and Kenton Corum, "Impacto da Políticas Agrárias no Tamanho das Propriedades. Um Estudo no Município de Caruaru no Agreste de Pernambuco," Boletim Econômico, 3, 1975, pp. 21, 22.

32. Ibid., p. 25.

33. Ibid., p. 27.

34. For an extensive discussion of agricultural development in Brazil using this approach, see G. Edward Schuh, The Agricultural Development of Brazil (New York: Praeger, 1970). Two Brazilian sources which provide comprehensive discussions from this perspective are IPES, A Reforma Agrária, and Ben Hur Raposo, A Reforma Agrária para o Brasil (Rio de Janeiro: Fundo de Cultura, 1965). Raposo worked for the landowners' confederation at the time the book was written.

35. Young and Corum, p. 27.

36. Peter Dorner, "Needed Redirection in Economic Analysis," in Peter Dorner, editor, Land Reform in Latin America: Issues and Cases (Madison, Wisconsin: Land Economics, 1971), p. 11.

37. Ibid., p. 15.

38. Baer, p. 47.

Appendix: Note on Sources

INTERVIEWS

As noted in the Preface, interviews for this study were conducted with a promise of confidentiality and anonymity, and are therefore not listed. It is possible, however, to indicate the scope and range of the interviews I conducted.

I interviewed sixty-eight individuals between January and October 1969, several of them more than once. To obtain as broad and complete a picture as possible of political and social group participation in the agrarian issue, I interviewed minister of state, administrators, senators, federal deputies, and political party leaders associated with both the Goulart and the Castelo Branco governments. I also conducted interviews with officials and members of the national confederations of agriculture, industry, and commerce, and with those of state federations in São Paulo, Guanabara, and Rio Grande do Sul. Finally, my interviews included discussions with leaders in agricultural workers' syndicates, with representatives of the Catholic church, and with military officers.

CONTENT ANALYSIS OF THE AGRARIAN DEBATE IN THE CHAMBER OF DEPUTIES

The universe consisted of 189 deputies who participated in the congressional debate on land reform for the three year period of 1962-1964. The content of every deputy's speeches and remarks on the agrarian issue was scanned for attitudinal information and classified according to the code which follows. Ordinal ranking was used for items 2 and 5-9. The primary purpose of the analysis was to obtain an aggregate view of particular attitudinal characteristics, and in certain instances measures of association (Gamma and Lambda) between key attitudes.

Code

1. State which the deputy represents.

2. Political party affiliation.

3. Number of times the deputy spoke on agrarian issue in 1962, 1963, 1964.

4. Introduced agrarian legislation (n.a., no, yes).

5. Perception of issue; evaluation of problem (n.a., no, yes):

    a. problem exists

    b. problem is economic

    c. problem is social

    d. problem is cultural

    e. problem is nation-wide

    f. problem is regional

    g. problem is a communist plot

    h. problem is artificially created by politicians to gain power.

6. Attitude toward specific measures (n.a., no, yes):

    a. favors credit programs

    b. favors extension services

    c. favors colonization programs

    d. favors progressive taxation

    e. favors forced leasing of land

    f. favors expropriation of idle land payable in cash

    g. favors expropriation of idle land payable in bonds

7. Attitude toward amending constitution (n.a., no, yes):

    a. in principle against any change

    b. against any changes affecting property

c. for, if for good social reason

d. for, if "the people demand it"

8. Political orientation to land reform issue (n.a., no, yes):

a. land reform necessary regardless of political circumstances

b. land reform undesirable, regardless of political circumstances

c. land reform is as desirable as the government in power at the time

d. President Goulart can be trusted with a constitutional amendment and land reform law

e. President Castelo Branco can be trusted with a constitutional amendment and land reform law

9. Reaction to specific legislative measures (n.a., against, for):

a. Brizola bill

b. Goulart-PTB amendment proposal and land bill

c. PSD-PTB compromise

d. Milton Campos bill

e. Badra bill

f. Estatuto da Terra

Glossary of Brazilian Terms and Acronyms

<u>bossa nova</u>: left wing of the UDN

<u>bachareis</u>: liberal intellectuals (identified with the UDN)

<u>camponês</u>: farmer, peasant, agricultural worker, countryman

<u>carioca</u>: native of the city of Rio de Janeiro

CNA: National Confederation of Agriculture (before 1966, the CRB)

<u>compactos</u>: radical wing of the PTB

<u>coronel</u>: rural political boss

CRB: Brazilian Rural Confederation (in 1966 became the CNA)

<u>Estado Nôvo</u>: literally "New State," a neofascist regime established by Getúlio Vargas 1937-45.

<u>fazendeiro</u>: land owner, usually understood to be a large property owner

<u>gaucho</u>: native of the state of Rio Grande do Sul

IBAD: Brazilian Institute for Democratic Action (private pressure group)

IBRA: Brazilian Agrarian Reform Institute

INCRA: National Institute of Colonization and Agrarian Reform

INDA: Brazilian Agrarian Development Institute

IPES: Institute for Social Research and Studies (private pressure group)

<u>ligas camponesas</u>: "peasant" leagues (see <u>camponês</u>, above) established by Francisco Julião.

<u>mineiro</u>: native of the state of Minas Gerais

<u>município</u>: local government unit below state level, roughly comparable to a municipal district.

<u>paulista</u>: native of the state of São Paulo

pelego: literally, sheepskin placed under a saddle. Colloquially used for more or less covert government agent or lackey in labor union.

pessedista: member of the PSD

petebista: member of the PTB

poder moderador: moderating, or mediating power of the emperor.

PSD: Social Democratic Party

PTB: Brazilian Labor Party

SUDENE: Superintendency for the Development of the Northeast

SUPRA: Superintendency for Agrarian Reform

udenista: member of the UDN

UDN: National Democratic Union

Bibliography

BRAZILIAN PUBLIC DOCUMENTS

Câmara dos Deputados. Anais da Câmara dos Deputados. Rio de Janeiro: Congresso Nacional, 1962-1964.

Congresso Nacional. Diario do Congresso Nacional. Rio de Janeiro: Congresso Nacional, 1962-1964.

Decreto n. 74,794 de 29 out. 74. Programa de Desenvolvimento de Areas Integradas do Nordeste. POLONORDESTE. Exposição de Motivos Interministerial n. 269-B, de 29 de outubro de 1974.

Instituto Brasileiro de Geografia e Estatística. Anuário Estatístico do Brasil. Rio de Janeiro: IBGE, 1954-1964.

______. Projeto do II Plano Nacional de Desenvolvimento, PND, 1975-1979. Rio de Janeiro: IBGE, 1974.

______. Sinopse Estatística do Brasil, 1975. Rio de Janeiro: IBGE, 1975.

Instituto Brasileiro de Reforma Agrária. As Areas Prioritárias. Decretos. Rio de Janeiro: IBRA, n.d.

______. Encôntro Sobre Ocupação do Territorio. Rio de Janeiro: IBRA, 1967.

______. Estrutura Agrária Brasileira. Rio de Janeiro, IBRA, 1967.

______. O ITR Calculado. Rio de Janeiro: IBRA, 1966.

______. Regulamento Geral. Decreto No. 55.889 de 31 de marco de 1965. Rio de Janeiro: IBRA, 1965.

_______. "Síntese das Principais Realizações, 1967/1968." Typescript.

Instituto Brasileiro de Reforma Agrária Regional/Rio Grande do Sul. Realidade Agrária do Rio Grande do Sul. Pôrto Alegre: IBRAR/RS, 1969.

Ministerio de Agricultura. Instituto Nacional de Colonização e Reforma Agrária. Relatôrio Anual, 1973. Rio de Janeiro: INCRA, 1973.

_______. Instituto Nacional de Desenvolvimento Agrário. Estatuto da Terra. Lei N. 4.504 de 30 de Novembro de 1964. Departamento de Imprenta Nacional, 1965.

Ministério de Planejamento e Coordenação Econômica. Programa de Ação Econômica do Govêrno, 1964-1966. Rio de Janeiro: Civilização Brasileira, 1972.

Monteiro Filho, Armando. Anteprojeto de Reforma Agrária. Rio de Janeiro: Ministério de Agricultura, Serviço de Informação Agrícola, 1962.

Senado. Anais do Senado. Rio de Janeiro: Congresso Nacional, 1962-1964.

NEWSPAPERS AND JOURNALS CONSULTED

Correio da Manhã (CM), 1962-1965.

Estado de São Paulo, select issues.

Folha de São Paulo, select issues.

Gleba, 1958-1969.

Jornal do Brasil (JB), 1961-1964.

Jornal do Comércio, select issues.

Tribuna da Imprensa, select issues.

Visão, 1961-1966.

UNPUBLISHED SOURCES

Borges, Thomas Pompeu de Accioly. "Novos Rumos para a Reforma

Agrária Brasileira." Internal document of the Grupo de Trabalho sobre Reforma Agrária. Rio de Janeiro, 1968. Typescript.

_______. "O Estatuto da Terra." Perguntas Formuladas por T. Pompeu Accioly Borges ao Dr. Paulo Assis Ribeiro, Presidente do IBRA, por Ocasião de sua Conferência no Club de Engenharia, o Dia 12 de Maio de 1966. Mimeographed.

Britto, Flavio da Costa. Relatôrio das Atividades da Confederação Nacional de Agricultura em 1968. Brasília, D.F. 1969. Mimeographed.

Cavalcanti, Amaro. "Cadastro Rural e Crédito Agrícola." Recife: Centro Sulamericano de Credito Agrícola, 1958. Mimeographed.

Confederação Nacional de Agricultura. "A Agricultura Brasileira." Mimeographed, 1969.

Confederação Rural Brasileira. Relatôrio das Atividades em 1965. Rio de Janeiro, 1965. Mimeographed.

_______. "Sindicalização Rural." Rio de Janeiro, n.d. Mimeographed.

Federação dos Trabalhadores na Agricultura Gauchos. Carta de Reivindicações do IV Congresso Estadual. Pôrto Alegre, 12 a 14 de Julho de 1969. Mimeographed.

_______. "O Clero e a Frente Agrária Gaucha." Pôrto Alegre, n.d. Mimeographed.

Lamounier, Bolivar. "Ideology and Authoritarian Regimes: Theoretical Perspectives and a Study of the Brazilian Case." Ph.D. dissertation, UCLA, 1974.

Leite, Edgar Teixeira. "Direito Agrário e Justiça Rural na Renovação Agrícola do Brasil." Conferência pronunciada no Instituto dos Advogados do Brasil. Rio de Janeiro, 1969. Mimeographed.

_______. "Reforma Agrária. Destinação Econômica e Social da Terra." Observações sobre o Anteprojeto da Comissão Especial. Rio de Janeiro: Conselho Nacional de Economia, n.d. Mimeographed.

Menges, Constantine. "The Politics of Agrarian Reform in Chile." Ph.D. dissertation. Columbia University, 1969.

Meinberg, Iris. "Plano de Trabalho (1967--1968--1969)

Apresentado pelo Presidente Iris Meinberg ao Conselho de Representantes." Rio de Janeiro: CNA, 1967. Mimeographed.

Peterson, Phyllis Jane. "Brazilian Political Parties: Formation, Organization and Leadership, 1945-1959." Ph.D. dissertation, University of Michigan, 1962.

Ribeiro, Paulo Assis. Conferência no Conselho Nacional de Economia. Rio de Janeiro, 1966. Mimeographed.

______. "Implantação da Reforma Agrária." Relatôrio de Abril 1964--Março 1967. Rio de Janeiro, 1967. Mimeographed.

Schilling, Arno. "Sindicalização Rural." Pôrto Alegre, 1969. Mimeographed.

Wilkie, Mary E. "A Report on the Rural Syndicates in Pernambuco." Rio de Janeiro: Centro de Pesquisas em Ciências Sociais, 1964. Mimeographed.

OTHER WORKS

Alexander, Robert J. "Nature and Progress of Agrarian Reform in Latin America." Journal of Economic History, No. 23 (December 1963). Pp. 559-73.

Alvarenza, Octavio Mello. "Justiça Agrária, Considerações Estruturais, Face a Realidade Brasileira." Revista do Direito Agrário 1(1973): 47--51.

Andrade, Manuel Correia de. A Terra e o Homem no Nordeste. São Paulo: Editôra Brasiliense, 1963.

Baer, Werner. Industrialization and Economic Development in Brazil. Homewood, Ill.: 1965.

Baklanoff, Eric N., ed. New Perspectives of Brazil. Nashville: Vanderbilt University Press, 1966.

Barraclough, Solon L. and Domike, Arthur L. "Agrarian Structures in Seven Latin American Countries." Land Economics 42(1966): 391-424.

Barros, Enrique de. A Estrutura Agrária como Obstáculo a Ação Agronômica. A Reforma Agrária como Problema Econômico. São Paulo: Escola de Sociologia e Política de São Paulo, 1954.

Beltrão, Hélio. A Revolução e o Desenvolvimento. Aula inaugural dos cursos da Escola Superior de Guerra. Rio de Janeiro: IBGE, 1969.

Borba, Lauro. Organização da Vida Rural. Recife: Federação das Associações Rurais do Estado de Pernambuco, 1952.

Callado, Antônio. Os Industriais da Seca e os "Galileus" de Pernambuco. Rio de Janeiro: Civilização Brasileira, 1960.

Campanhôle, Adriano, ed., Consolidação das Leis do Trabalho e Legislação Complementar. São Paulo: Editôra Atlas, 1966.

Campanhôle, Adriano, ed., Legislação Agrária. São Paulo: Atlas, 1969.

Campanhôle, Adriano, and Campanhole, Hilton Lôbo. Legislação Agrária. 6th ed. São Paulo: Editora Atlas, 1974.

Campos, Roberto de Oliveira. Política Econômica e Mitos Políticos. Rio de Janeiro: APEC, 1965.

Cardoso, Fernando Henrique. Autoritarismo e Democratização. Rio de Janeiro: Paz e Terra, 1975.

_______. "Tensões Sociais no Campo e Reforma Agrária." Revista Brasileira de Estudos Políticos. N. 12 (outubro 1961). Pp. 7-26.

Cehelsky, Marta. "A Case Study in Urbanization: Brazil." Population and Urbanization Problems of Latin America. Edited by Philip B. Taylor and Sam Schulman. Houston: University of Houston, 1971.

_______. "Redistributive Policy and Agrarian Reform." Contemporary Brazil: Issues in Economic and Political Development. Edited by H. Jon Rosenbaum and William G. Tyler. New York: Praeger, 1972.

Cesarino Júnior, A.F. "Conceito de Trabalhador Rural para Efeito de Enquadramento Sindical." Jurídica, No. 100 (janeiro--março, 1968).

Cline, William R. Economic Consequences of a Land Reform in Brazil. London: North-Holland Publishing Company, 1970.

Comité Interamericano sobre Desarrollo Agrário. Land Tenure Conditions and Socio-Economic Development in Brazil. Washington, D.C.: Pan American Union, 1963.

Confederação Nacional de Agricultura. Novas Sugestões ao Govêrno da República. Serie Problemas Gerais. Rio de Janeiro:

Irmãos Di Giorgio, 1967.

______. Sistema Tributário Nacional: Lei No. 5.172 de 25/10/66. Rio de Janeiro: CNA, n.d.

______. Confederação Nacional dos Trabalhadores na Agricultura. Diretrizes das Classes Patronais e Trabalhadoras. Rio de Janeiro, 1969.

Confederação Rural Brasileira. "A Agricultura Brasileira. Diretrizes para um Plano de Ação." Memorial da CRB ao Exmo. Senhor Presidente da Republica, Doutor Jânio da Silva Quadros. Gleba, (Março 1961).

______. Política Rural. Rio de Janeiro, 1968.

______. "Quarta Conferência Rural." Rio de Janeiro: Gleba, 1962.

______. (Confederação Nacional de Agricultura). Sindicalização Rural. Rio de Janeiro: CRB, n.d.

Corbisier, Roland. Reforma ou Revolução? Rio de Janeiro: Civilização Brasileira, 1968.

Cunha, Euclides da. Rebellion in the Backlands. Chicago: University of Chicago Press, 1944.

Da Silva, José Gomes. A Reforma Agrária no Brasil. Rio de Janeiro: Zahar Editores, 1971.

Dean, Warren Kempton. The Industrialization of Sao Paulo, 1880-1945. Austin: The University of Texas Press, 1969.

______. "The Problem of the Latifundia in Nineteenth Century Brazil." Hispanic American Historical Review, (November, 1971).

Delfim Neto, Antônio. "Agricultura e Desenvolvimento." Mundo Econômico 10, (1967).

Diegues Júnior, Manuel. População e Açucar no Nordeste do Brasil. Rio de Janeiro: Comissão Nacional de Alimentação, 1965.

______. População e Propriedade da Terra no Brasil. Washington, D.C.: Pan American Union, 1959.

Dorner, Peter, ed. Land Reform in Latin America: Issues and Cases. Madison, Wisconsin: Land Economics, 1971.

Dulles, John W.F. Vargas of Brazil: A Political Biography. Austin: The University of Texas Press, 1967.

Dutra, Eloy. IBAD, Sigla da Corrupção. Rio de Janeiro: Civilização Brasileira, 1963.

Eisenstadt, S.M. The Political Systems of Empires. New York: The Free Press, 1969.

Ellis, Howard S. The Economy of Brazil. Berkeley: University of California Press, 1969.

Erickson, Kenneth P. The Brazilian Corporative State and Working Class Politics. Berkeley, University of California Press, 1977.

______. "Corporatism and Labor in Development." Contemporary Brazil: Issues in Economic and Political Development. Edited by H. Jon Rosenbaum and William G. Tyler. New York: Praeger, 1972.

Faoro, Raymundo. Os Donos do Poder. Pôrto Alegre: Editorial Globo, 1958.

Feder, Ernst. The Rape of the Peasantry. New York: Doubleday, 1971.

Federação dos Trabalhadores na Agricultura no Rio Grande do Sul. FETAG. História/Trabalho/Preocupações. Pôrto Alegre, 1969.

Federação dos Trabalhadores na Agricultura Gauchos. Relatôrio. Pôrto Alegre: FETAG, 1968.

Fiechter, Georges-Andre. Brazil Since 1964: Modernization Under a Military Regime. New York: John Wiley, 1975.

Frente Agrária Gaucha. Verdade e Justiça para o Homem do Campo. Pôrto Alegre, n.d.

Freyre, Gilberto. Ordem e Progresso. Rio de Janeiro: Editôra José Olympio, 1959.

Furtado, Celso. Análise do Modelo Brasileiro. Rio de Janeiro: Civilização Brasileira, 1972.

______. The Economic Growth of Brazil. Translated by Ricardo W. de Aguiar and Eric Charles Drysdale. Berkeley: University of California Press, 1965.

Galjert, Benno. "Class and 'Following' in Rural Brazil."

América Latina 7 (1964): 3-24.

Geisel, Ernesto. "O Homem e o Campo." Planejamento e Desenvolvimento 4(1976): 26-31.

Graham, Richard. "Landowners and the Overthrow of the Empire." Luso-Brazilian Review 7 (1970): 44-56.

Guimarães, Alberto Passos. Quatro Séculos de Latifúndio. Rio de Janeiro: Pax e Terra, 1968.

Hirschman, Albert O. Journeys Toward Progress. New York: Doubleday, 1965.

Horowitz, Irving Louis. Revolution in Brazil. New York: Dutton, 1964.

Huizer, Gerrit. "Some Notes on Community Development and Social Research." América Latina, 8 (1965): 128-44.

Huntington, Samuel. Political Order in Changing Societies. New Haven: Yale University Press, 1968.

_______, and Moore, Clement H. Authoritarian Politics in Modern Society. New York: Basic Books, 1970.

Ianni, Octavio. O Colapso do Populismo no Brasil. Rio de Janeiro: Civilização Brasileira, 1968.

_______. "A Constituição do Proletariado Agrícola no Brasil." Revista Brasileira de Estudos Políticos 12 (1961): 27-46.

_______. Estado e Capitalismo. Rio de Janeiro: Civilização Brasileiro, 1965.

_______, et al. Política e Revolução Social no Brasil. Rio de Janeiro: Civilização Brasileira, 1964.

Institute for the Comparative Study of Political Systems. Edited by Ronald Schneider, Charles Daugherty, and James Rowe. Brazil Election Factbook. Washington, D.C.: Operations and Policy Research, 1965.

Instituto Brasileiro de Ação Democrática. Recomendações sobre Reforma Agrária. Rio de Janeiro: IBAD, 1961.

Instituto de Ciências Socias. Bibliografia sobre Reforma Agrária. Rio de Janeiro: Universidade do Brasil, 1962.

Instituto de Pesquisas e Estudos Sociais. A Reforma Agrária: Problemas, Bases, e Soluções. Rio de Janeiro: IPES, 1964.

Ionescu, Ghita, and Gellner, Ernest, eds. Populism, its Meanings and National Characteristics. London: Weidenfeld and Nicolson, 1969.

Jaguaribe, Helio. "A Crise Brasileira." Cadernos de Nosso Tempo 1 (1953): 120-60.

______. Economic and Political Development. Translated by Suzette Macedo. Cambridge, Massachusetts: Harvard University Press, 1968.

Julião, Francisco, ed. Ligas Camponesas: Outubro 1962-Abril 1964. Cuernavaca: CIDOC, 1969.

Kaufman, Robert. The Chilean Political Right and Agrarian Reform. Resistance and Moderation. Washington, D.C.: ICOPS, 1967.

______. The Politics of Land Reform in Chile, 1950-1970. Public Policy, Political Institutions, and Social Change. Cambridge, Mass.: Harvard University Press, 1972.

Keller, Suzanne. Beyond the Ruling Class. New York: Random House, 1964.

Landsberger, Henry, A., ed. Latin American Peasant Movements. Ithaca, N.Y.: Cornell University Press, 1969.

Lapalombara, Joseph. "The Utility and Limitations of Interest Group Theory in Non-American Field Situations." Journal of Politics, XXII (February, 1960).

Leal, Victor Nunes. Coronelismo, Enxada e Voto. Rio de Janeiro: Livraria Forense, 1949.

Leeds, Anthony. "Brazilian Careers and Social Structure: An Evolutionary Model and Case History." American Anthropologist 66, Part I (1964): 1321-47.

Leite, Edgar Teixeira. "Aspectos do Complexo Agrário Brasileiro." Carta Mensal do Conselho Técnico da Confederação Nacional da Industria 180 (1970).

______. "Aspectos da Sindicalização Rural no Brasil." Jurídica, XXXI (abril-junho, 1966).

______. "O Problema da Terra no Brasil." Revista Brasileira de Geografia. (abril-junho, 1959).

______. A Revolução Agrícola pela Tecnificação do Homem Rural. Rio de Janeiro: Confederação Nacional de Agricultura, 1967.

Leff, Nathaniel. *Economic Policy-Making and Development in Brazil, 1947-1964*. New York: Wiley, 1968.

Levine, Robert M. *The Vargas Regime: The Critical Years, 1934-1938*. New York: Columbia University Press, 1970.

Linz, Juan. "An Authoritarian Regime: Spain." In *Cleavages, Ideologies and Party Systems*. Edited by Erik Allardt and Yrjo Littune. Helsinki, 1964.

Lopes, Juarez R.B. *A Crise do Brasil Arcáico*. São Paulo: Difusão Européia do Livro, 1967.

______. *Desenvolvimento e Mudança Social*. São Paulo: Companhia Editôra Nacional, 1968.

Love, Joseph L. *Rio Grande do Sul and Brazilian Regionalism, 1882-1930*. Stanford, California: Stanford University Press, 1971.

Lowi, Theodore. "American Business, Public Policy, Case Studies, and Political Theory." *World Politics*, 4(1964).

Ludwig, Armin D., and Taylor, Harry W. *Brazil's New Agrarian Reform. An Evaluation of its Property Classification and Tax Systems*. New York: Praeger, 1969.

Maia, J. Motta. "O Estatuto da Terra. Apreciação e Texto." *Jurídica* 29(1964).

Marcondes, J.V. Freitas. "O Sindicalismo Rural e a Reforma Agrária." *Revista Brasileira de Estudos Políticos* 20(1966): 49-58.

Martins, Joaó de Sousa. *A Imigração e a Crise do Brasil Agrário*. São Paulo: Editôra Pioneira, 1973.

Meinberg, Iris. "São Empresarios o Pequeno Proprietário, O Arrendatário e o Parceiro." *Gleba* 13(1967).

Moore, Barrington. *The Social Origins of Dictatorship and Democracy. Lord and Peasant in the Making of the Modern World*. Boston: Beacon Press, 1966.

Pedreira, Fernando. *Março 31. Civis e Militares no Processo da Crise Brasileira*. Rio de Janeiro: José Alvaro, 1964.

Pereira, Osny Duarte. *A Constituição Federal e Suas Modificações Incorporadas ao Texto*. Rio de Janeiro; Civilização Brasileira, 1966.

______. "O Estatuto de Reforma Agrária." Revista Civilização Brasileira 1(1965): 24-44.

Petras, James F. and La Porte Jr., Robert. Cultivating Revolution. The United States and Agrarian Reform. New York: Random House, 1971.

Prado Jr., Caio. "Contribuição para a Análise da Questão Agrária no Brasil." Revista Brasiliense 28(1960): 165-238.

______. "O Estatuto do Trabalhador Rural." Revista Brasil--iense 47(1963): 1-13.

______. História Econômica do Brasil. 11th edition. São Paulo: Editôra Brasiliense, 1969.

Puggina, Adolpho. Reforma Agrária. A Reforma das Reformas. Pôrto Alegre: FETAG, 1968.

Raposo, Ben Hur. A Reforma Agrária para o Brasil. Rio de Janeiro: Fundo de Cultura, 1965.

Ribeiro, Paulo de Assis. Conferência Realizada no Conselho Nacional de Economia. Rio de Janeiro: IBRA, 1966.

Rodriguez, Dom Orlando, et al. Declaração do Morro Alto. Programa de Política Agrária Conforme os Princípios de Reforma Agrária, Questão de Consciência. São Paulo: Editôra Vera Cruz, 1964.

______. Reforma Agrária, Questão de Consciência. São Paulo: Editôra Vera Cruz, 1960.

Roett, Riordan, editor. Brazil in the Seventies. Washington, D.C.: American Enterprise Institute for Public Policy Research, 1976,

______, editor. Brazil in the Sixties. Nashville, Tenn.: Vanderbilt University Press, 1972.

Rokeach, Milton. Beliefs, Attitudes, and Values. San Francisco: Jossey-Bass, 1969.

Rustow, Dankwart A. A World of Nations. Washington, D.C.: The Brookings Institution, 1967.

Sampaio, Pericles. "Previdência Rural: Linhas Gerais, Aspectos Jurídicos." Revista Brasileira de Estudos Políticos 35(1973): 69-79.

Santos, Arthur Pio dos. "PROTERRA: Reforma Agrária Consentida." Revista do Direito Agrário 1(1973): 9-12.

Schattschneider, E.E. The Semi-Sovereign People. A Realist's View of Democracy in America. New York: Holt, Rinehart, and Winston, 1960.

Scherer, Cardeal D. Vicente. A Questão Agrária. Pôrto Alegre, n.d.

Schmitter, Philippe C. Interest Conflict and Political Change in Brazil. Stanford, California: Stanford University Press, 1971.

Schneider, Ronald M. Brazil. Foreign Policy of a Future World Power. Boulder, Colorado: Westview Press, 1976.

_______. The Political System of Brazil. Emergence of a "Modernizing" Authoritarian Regime. New York: Columbia University Press, 1971.

Schuh, G. Edward, in collaboration with Eliseu Roberto Alves. The Agricultural Development of Brazil. New York: Praeger, 1970.

Siekman, Philip. "When Executives Turned Revolutionaries." Fortune, September, 1964.

Silva, José Gomes da. A Reforma Agrária no Brasil. Frustração Camponesa ou Instrumento de Desenvolvimento. Rio de Janeiro: Zahar Editores, 1971.

Silva, Victor da, and Buescu, Mircea. Dez Anos de Renovação Econômica. Rio de Janeiro: APEC, 1974.

Simonsen, Mario Henrique. A Nova Economia Brasileira. Rio de Janeiro: Livraria José Olympio, 1974.

Singer, Paulo. Desenvolvimento Econômico e Evolução Urbana. São Paulo: Universidade de São Paulo, 1968.

Skidmore, Thomas E. Politics in Brazil, 1930-1964. New York: Oxford University Press, 1967.

Smith, T. Lynn, editor. Agrarian Reform in Latin America. New York: Alfred A Knopf, 1965.

Stavenhagen, Rodolfo, editor. Agrarian Problems and Peasant Movements in Latin America. New York: Doubleday, 1970.

Stein, Stanley. Vassouras, A Brazilian Coffee County, 1850-1900. Cambridge, Massachusetts: Harvard University Press, 1957.

Stepan, Alfred, editor. Authoritarian Brazil: Origins, Policies, and Future. New Haven: Yale University Press, 1973.

______. The Military in Politics. Changing Patterns in Brazil. Princeton, New Jersey: Princeton University Press, 1971.

Tavares, Assis. "Caio Prado e a Teoria da Revolução Brasileira." Revista Civilização Brasileira 11-12(1967): 48-80.

Torres, João Camilo de Oliveira. A Democrácia Coroada. Rio de Janeiro: Livraria José Olympio, 1957.

______. Estratificação Social no Brasil. São Paulo: Difusão Européia do Livro, 1965.

Veliz, Claudio, editor. Obstacles to Change in Latin America. New York: Oxford University Press, 1965.

Vera, Nestor. "O Congresso Camponês em Belo Horizonte." Revista Brasiliense. 39(1962): 499.

Viana Filho, Luis. O Govêrno Castelo Branco. Rio de Janeiro: Livraria José Olympio, 1975.

Vinhas, M. Problemas Agrario-Camponeses dc Brasil. Rio de Janeiro: Civilização Brasileira, 1968.

Warriner, Doreen. Land Reform in Principle and Practice. London: Clarendon Press, 1969.

Wirth, John. The Politics of Brazilian Development, 1930-1954. Stanford, California: Stanford University Press, 1970.

Young, Douglas, and Corum, Kenton. "Impacto das Políticas Agrárias no Tamanho das Propriedades. Um Estudo no Município de Caruaru no Nordeste de Pernambuco." Boletim Econômico 3(1975): 21-33.

Index

Afonso, Almino, 87, 91
Agrarian policy
    in Triennial Plan, 82, 140
    Kubitschek and, 32-33
    revolutionary government and, 198-226
    similarities of agrarian bills and, 68-73
    social disorder and, 92-94, 97-98
    states and, 83-85, 184-185
    success of, 197-198
    Vargas and, 26-28
    See also Regionalism
Agrarian reform bills compared, 68-73
Agricultural Revision Law of São Paulo, 83-84
Agricultural Society of Planters and Cattle Ranchers of Pernambuco (SAPP), 41
Agriculture
    and politics, 2, 17, 21-22, 32-33, 39-43, 80, 166-168, 174
    occupational structure in, 44
    social conditions in, 36-37
    See also Patrimonialism; Regionalism
Aleixo, Pedro, 151
Amendment, 67-68, 83-90, 92, 131, 135, 142
    as measure of ideological conviction, 181-186
    Castelo and Goulart, contrasted, 103-104, 203
    constitution of 1946 and land reform, 73-74
    Goulart-PTB, 96, 145, 148-153, 186, 189-191
    No. 18 (1965), 210-211
    No. 5 (1961), 84, 160, 210
    No. 10 (1964), approved, 112, 157
    procedure, 75-76

PSD-mineiro proposal, 143, 145-146
ARENA, See National Renovation Alliance
Armed forces, See Military
Arrais, Miguel, 103
Authoritarian rule, 15, 22 225-230
and agrarian issue, 34, 226
Cartorial State and, 24-25
changes of regime in, 15-17
Congress and, 119, 161
patrimonialism and, 16-21 80-86, 225
populism as an aspect of, 30, 77
theories of, 4-5
See also Corporatism; Military

Badra, Aniz, 107, 150
agrarian reform bill of, 107, 111, 151, 156-157, 190-191
Baer, Werner, 220
Barros, Adhemar de, 148
Basic Reforms, Program of, 82-83, 133, 139, 198
Borges, Thomas Pompeu Accioli, 55
bossa nova, 136-137, 141, 175
See also National Democratic Union
Brazilian Communist Party (PCB), 41-42, 47
and rural labor organization, 42, 47
Brazilian Institute of Agrarian Development, 204, 207, 217, 218
Brazilian Institute of Agrarian Reform, 102, 204, 206, 209, 217, 218, 223
Brazilian Labor Party, 81, 96, 140-155 passim, 150, 152
Goulart, 78, 80, 91, 110, 125, 138, 191, 203
origins of, 29, 124
voting behavior on Goulart amendment and, 184, 185, 187-188, 190-191
Brazilian Rural Confederation, 27, 45, 47-48, 49-51, 85, 108
Brazilian Rural Society, 49
Brizola, Leonel, 43, 68, 81, 83, 90, 92, 95, 134, 138, 143
Bulhões, Octávio, 106
Bureaucracy
as organ of social control, 20
in the Cartorial State, 23-24
patrimonial, 16-17

Cabo eleitoral, 29

Câmara, Dom Helder, 55
Camponeses, 34, 37, 45, 48, 69
and union organizaton, 42, 46
and Land Statute, 209-211
See also Ligas Camponesas
Campos, Milton, 69, 86, 95, 110, 135
agrarian reform bill, 86, 95, 106-107, 135-139, 148-150
Campos, Roberto, 101, 106, 108, 110, 157
Capanema, Gustavo, 142, 143
Carli, Gileno de, 109-110, 137
Carta de Brasília, 138
Carta de Princípios, 136, 138
Cartorial State, 24-25
Caruso, João, 89-90
Carvalho, Ultimo de, 112, 158, 160, 184, 187
Castelo Branco, Humberto
and constitutional amendment, 157
and Congress, 108-109, 111-113, 155-159
and landowners, 106-108
and land reform policy compared to Goulart, 67-68, 75-76, 104-106, 121-122, 184-186, 203
development goals of, 99-102, 113, 197, 203-205
Catholic church, 42, 54, 103
Chaves, Pacheco, 111, 159
Clientelism, 6, 16, 194
and political parties, 29-30, 124-125, 175
interest group articulation and, 128-200
Communist party, See Brazilian Communist Party
CONCLAP, See Superior Council of Producing Classes
Congress, 130-131, 153-168
and attitudes toward land reform policy, 179-186
and relations with Castelo, 155-159
and relations with Goulart, 93-96
interest group activity in, 128-129
legislative process and, 74-76
reduction of powers of, 100-101
See also Regionalism
Consolidated Labor Code, 25, 59 fn.
Corporatism
and interest group behavior, 128, 200
and political control, 205, 226-228
and statist ethic, 17, 26, 30, 200-202

as source of authority, 32
federated interest structure in, 25
institutional crisis of, 77
Vargas and development of, 201
See also Syndicalism
Coroneis (Coronelismo), 22, 26, 28-29, 167, 176, 202
Costa e Silva, Arthur, 54, 109
Cunha, Bocayuva, 151, 153

Dantas, Santiago, 87, 91
Declaration of Goiânia, 85
Delfim Neto, Antônio, 53, 109
Democratic Parliamentary Coalition, (ADP) 81
Dos Prazares, José, 41

Economic Development (modernization)
and cartorialism, 24-25
and import substitution policy, 31-32, 220
land reform issue in, 34-39, 48, 57
military governments and, 101-103, 105-106, 198, 207, 214, 219-224, 227-230
of agrarian sector, 17, 32, 34, 39, 205
Vargas and, 23-27, 31

Electoral system, 28-32
and mass mobilization, 120, 125
coalitions in, 175
elite strategy in, 32
regional bias of, 167
under Empire, 21
under Second Republic, 28-29, 34
See also Clientelism, Populism
Elites
and interest group effectiveness, 200
and policy process, 198-200, 226-227
during revolutionary period, 215
political control by, 98, 227
Estado Nôvo, 26-28
Executive Group for Agrarian Reform, 217-218
Expropriation, 67-68, 73, 85-90 passim, 131, 135, 142
Castelo and, 206-211
Goulart decree on, 98, 140-153, 186-190, 154
in Rio Grande do Sul, 92
Institutional Act No.9 and, 215-216
Since 166, 223

Ferrari, Fernando, 44, 81
Furtado, Celso, 87, 91, 140

Garrastazú Médici, Emílio, 54, 218
GERA, See Executive Group for Agrarian Reform
Goulart, João (Jango)
and Basic Reforms, 82-83
and conservative opposition, 56, 199-200
and military, 55
and Vargas, 76-79
charter of, 7, 76-79, 197-203
compared to Castelo, 67-68, 75-76, 104-106, 203
congressional relations and, 80, 85, 87-91, 121, 140, 143, 147-153, 186-189
during parliamentary regime, 51, 80-82
land reform bill of, 88-89, 140
populism as strategy of, 43-49, 80-81, 89, 92-95, 97-98, 125, 147, 154-155
relations with planter interests, 49-52, 85-89, 98, 106, 200
strategy in land reform, 199-202
Government Program of Action, 101

IBRA, See Brazilian Institute of Agrarian Reform
Imposto Territorial Rural, 210
INCRA, See National Institute for Colonization and Land Reform
INDA, See Brazilian Institute of Agrarian Development
Institutional Acts:
No. 1, 74-75, 100, 112
No. 2, 213
No. 3, 213
No. 5, 203, 214
No. 9, 215, 217
Interest groups
and cartorialism, 24-25
and economic decision making, 6-7
and foreign policy, 7-8
impact of populism and clientelism on, 127-128
impact on electoral system, 31, 127
in policy process, 8, 47-55, 128, 199-200
organization, 25, 27, 127-130
relation to party system, 122, 124

Julião de Paula, Francisco, 41, 46, 103
Kubitschek, Juscelino, 32, 137, 201, 212

Labor movement
and Goulart, 147
and populism, 48
protected by legislation, 25, 60 fn.
under Vargas, 25-26, 41, 124
Lacerda, Carlos, 93, 136
Land reform, *See* Agrarian policy; Amendment; Expropriation; Land Statute
Land reform bonds, 89, 104, 132, 140, 142, 208, 210, 216
Land Statute, 104, 112, 159-160, 190, 215-216, 221, 226
content of, 205-211
Land tax, 210-22, 215-216, 221-223
Land tenure pattern, 19, 35-38, 206, 223-225
Landed elites (fazendeiros, planter class)
and business elites, 52-53, 199
and Castelo, 57, 106-108
and Goulart, 89
and revolutionary policies, 198-200, 215, 222, 226-227
effectiveness as interest group, 47-53
power of, 17, 19,21-23, 26
reaction to agrarian policy, 47-50, 57, 142, 144, 174-175, 198-200, 226-228
Leme, Hugo, 106
Ligas camponesas, 41-42, 46-47, 63 fn., 103, 134, 173
Lott, Henrique Teixeira, 141

Mazilli, Ranieri, 139
Meinberg, Iris, 49
Mendes, João, 112, 130, 157, 159
Middle class
and revolution of 1964, 201, 222-225
cartorialism and, 24
in revolution of 1930, 23
political incorporation of, 40, 228
Military
and Castelo, 100-101, 105
and Goulart, 56, 76, 78, 82, 91, 93, 121, 198
and land reform, 55, 91-93, 198, 212, 216, 218, 221-226
and National War College (ESG), 101
and SUPRA, 97
and Vargas, 201
development plans of, 198, 214, 219-224, 228-229

in 1964 crisis, 227
linha dura of, 56, 212-214, 217
Milton Campos Commission, See Special Commission for Agrarian Reform
Moderating power, 16-20, 200
See also Patrimonialism

National Council on Agrarian Reform, 86
National Democratic Union
and Castelo, 109-112, 158-159, 188
and Goulart, 78, 80, 135-136, 188
attitudes toward land reform, 135-137, 141, 147-148, 156, 181, 184, 205
description of, 122, 175
distribution of seats in Congress, 125
origins, 29
National Institute for Colonization and Land Reform, 219, 221
National Liberation Front, 81
Neves, Tancredo, 86, 141, 151

Parliamentary regime, 51, 64 fn., 77, 135
limitations of, 133
plebiscite on, 80, 82, 86
Patrimonialism
and planter class, 53
continuity of, 225, 228
political parties and, 124
relationship of agrarian issue to, 34, 39
revival by Vargas of, 39-40
role of bureaucracy in, 16, 20
Peasants, See Camponeses
Peixoto, Amaral, 109-110, 137-138, 143
Pinheiro Neto, João, 94, 97, 190
Pinto, Carvalho, 83, 91
Pinto, José de Magelhaes, 135-136
Policy process
and institutional crisis, 77
Castelo strategy and, 197, 203-214
Goulart strategy and, 197-203
impact of patrimonialism, corporatism on, 31-32
political parties participation in, 192
president and, 6-9, 52
under revolutionary government, 100
under Second Republic, 28

Populism
and effect on stability, 125-127, 169
and institutional crisis, 77
and agrarian reform, 40, 92, 169, 177
and role in electoral system, 31-32, 125
and urban politics, 169, 173-174, 177
Goulart and, 92-94, 97, 121, 125
Kubitschek and, 32-34
urban labor and, 48
Presidency
and economic decision making, 6-7
and foreign policy, 7-8
and legislative process, 74-76
and policy process, 6-9, 76, 132, 186-190, 200-204
crisis of authority and, 77-78
interest groups and, 48-51, 128, 199-200
Program for Distribution of Land and Stimulus to Agroindustry in the North and Northeast (PROTERRA), 221
PSD, See Social Democratic Party
PTB, See Brazilian Labor Party

Quadros, Jânio, 49, 77, 78, 130, 153

Regionalism, 21-23, 84-85, 119-120, 166-175
municipalism as aspect of, 83-85, 108
See also Coroneis
Ribeiro, Paulo Assiz, 102, 107
Rodriguez, Mário Martíns, 148
Rural workers
and Goulart land reform bill, 140, 207
and revolutionary policy, 222, 229
Castelo consultation with, 108
occupational structure of, 40, 44-45
unionization of, 40-43, 47
Ruralist strategy, 84-85
Also see Regionalism

Sesmarias, 18-19
compared to Land Statute, 207
Silva, Amaury, 47
Social Democratic Party
and agrarian reform, 137-138, 141-143, 145-153, 184, 186, 205
and Castelo, 109-110,

158, 188
and distribution of seats in Congress, 125
and Goulart, 78, 80-81, 88, 96, 148-151, 188, 203, 212
as part of Democratic Parliamentary Action Coalition, 81
mineiro wing of, 142-143, 145, 149-150, 194
Special Commission for Agrarian Reform, 69, 83, 86, 113, 142, 143
SRB, See Brazilian Rural Society
SUDENE, See Superintendency of the Northeast
Superior Council of Producing Classes (CONCLAP), 57
SUPRA, See Superintendency of Agrarian Reform
Superintendency of Agrarian Reform, 69, 86, 89-91, 94, 97, 139, 154, 189
Syndicalism, 25, 27, 40, 45, 46
in agriculture, 27

Target Program (Programa de Metas) 32-33
Teixeira Leite, Edgar, 49
Triennial Plan, 87, 91, 140

UDN, See National Democratic Union
ULTAB, See Union of Agricultural Laborers and Workers
Union of Agricultural Laborers and Workers, 42, 47

Vargas, Getúlio
and cartorial state, 24
and corporatist political framework, 26-28, 201
and Goulart, 78-79, 200
and origins of party system, 122, 124
and regional interests, 120
labor strategy of, 25-26, 40
Viana, Aurélio, 111, 159

Workers' Renovation Movement, 186

For Product Safety Concerns and Information please contact our EU representative GPSR@taylorandfrancis.com Taylor & Francis Verlag GmbH, Kaufingerstraße 24, 80331 München, Germany

Batch number: 10726013

Printed by Printforce, the Netherlands